# Photography
## An Introduction
### A Guide to City & Guilds 9231 Photography

# Photography
## An Introduction
### A Guide to City & Guilds 9231 Photography

Dr C.J. Stratmann MSc, PhD, ARPS

**Longman Scientific & Technical**
Longman Group Limited
Longman House, Burnt Mill, Harlow
Essex CM20 2JE, England
*and Associated Companies throughout the world*



First published 1995

**British Library Cataloguing in Publication Data**
A catalogue entry for this title is available from the British Library

ISBN 0-582-23825-0

Set by 3 in 10½/13pt Bembo
Produced by Longman Singapore (Pte) Ltd
Printed in Singapore

# Contents

# Acknowledgements

The author would like to express his gratitude to Miss Tracy Preston for producing the originals of many of the excellent diagrams which appear in this book, to Mrs Jill Curry for typing the manuscript and to Messrs Mark and Gary Stratmann for invaluable advice. Thanks are also due to the able photographers who provided photographs. They are acknowledged, where appropriate, in the captions to the photographs. Unacknowledged photographs were taken by the author. Finally, grateful thanks are due to my wife for her unfailing encouragement (and patience), her discerning criticism of the photography, and her many useful suggestions.

# Introduction

This book is intended to provide a basic introduction to photography. It is particularly aimed at those who wish to take the most popular modules in the highly successful City & Guilds 9231 Photography scheme.

In addition it will provide a sound foundation for anyone wishing to proceed to study and produce photographs for the more advanced City & Guilds modules.

The particular syllabuses of the City & Guilds 9231 Photography Courses which are covered in detail comprise 9231–020 Starting Photography, 9231–030 Introduction to Black and White Photography, 9231–040 Introduction to Colour Photography, 9231–050 Portraiture and 9231–060 Photo Essay. The other presently available City & Guilds modules are listed in the appendix on page 207. As you will see, a very wide range of photographic techniques and fields are covered. City & Guilds publish a series of inexpensive, small pamphlets giving guidelines of the scheme, the various syllabuses and the requirements for each examination submission. All are based on practical work and written material. No formal written papers conducted under examination conditions are required. The scheme booklets are obtainable from the City & Guilds of London Institute, Publications Section, 76 Portland Place, London W1N 4AA; telephone 0171-278-2468.

The basic photography course provided by City & Guilds is the module 9231–020 Starting Photography. This module assumes that the student is a beginner and knows nothing about photography. The course, therefore, starts from very basic first principles, covering how the photographic image is formed, how cameras work and how to compose good pictures. Because the subject is very wide and covers a good deal of ground, it takes up the first eight chapters in this book. Details of the examination requirements for Starting Photography will be found in the Appendix. The basic module 9231–030, Introduction to Black and White Photography, requires the background provided in Chapters 1–8 and, in addition, Chapters 9 and 10 which deal respectively with film processing and printing and enlarging. Details of the examination requirements for

Introduction to Black and White Photography are given in the Appendix. The other basic module covered is 9231–040 Introduction to Colour Photography. This also calls for the basic theory of Chapters 1–8, and the more specialist needs of the colour photographer appear in Chapter 11. Details of the examination submission for Introduction to Colour Photography can also be found in the Appendix.

The City & Guilds advanced courses, of which Portraiture and Photo Essay are examples, assume that the photographer has a basic photographic background in theory and practice equivalent to being able to pass one of the introductory modules such as Starting Photography, Introduction to Black and White Photography and Introduction to Colour Photography. In Chapter 12 we cover the advanced module 9231–050 Portraiture, and in Chapter 13 the requirements of 9231–060 Photo Essay are discussed together with brief details of the closely related module 9231–061, Social Documentary Photography. Submission details for the modules 9231–050 and 9231–060 are given in the Appendix.

City & Guilds 9231 courses comprise ten two-hour classroom periods, usually weekly, conducted at a recognised City & Guilds centre. There are, however, some intensive courses offered and there are also Correspondence Schools offering 9231 courses. City & Guilds can provide a full list of centres offering these courses.

City & Guilds 9231 examinations are in the form of submissions of practical work plus appropriate written material. The exact requirements vary from syllabus to syllabus. However, in all cases, you will need to submit a *workbook* in addition to the photographs. Another strict requirement is that you must provide a self-evaluation of your work when it is finished. Your tutor is usually your examiner. Your submission will be marked by your tutor first of all using the special City & Guilds assessment form 9231/A1, marks being allocated according to City & Guilds suggestions and your own centre's emphasis. The marked submission will then be re-examined by an official City & Guilds verifier who will either agree with your tutor's marks or make appropriate changes in them.

This will be the final marking and at that point you will be notified of your results. The City & Guilds Certificate will follow in due course.

## The workbook

The easiest way to produce the workbook is to look upon it as a 'diary' or 'journal' of what you have done while studying the subject and producing the photographs. It can be quite brief and handwritten if you wish but it must be included if you want a good grading. Indeed, City & Guilds now place such importance on the workbook that there is a very real danger that candidates may fail if it is not included in their submissions.

In the workbook it is quite in order to include brief notes on what has been discussed in each class or on what you have actually studied. City & Guilds suggest that, for example, those students studying the Portraiture module could do well to visit art galleries and study portrait paintings. Brief notes of what was seen and learned can be included in the workbook. In addition, notes on what you intended to do when going out to take your pictures should be included together with a few notes on what you *actually* accomplished. As previously stated, if you regard the workbook as a diary and make entries regularly while working on the course, you will find nothing difficult or formidable about it.

## Self-evaluation

The self-evaluation requirement often seems a little daunting. However, all you really require to do is to look over your work with a critical eye when you have finished it, then consider how you might improve it if you had the opportunity to do the work again. Students are warned against writing 'this is all such good work that I cannot see how it could be improved'. There is always room for improvement and your experience gained in doing the work should enable you to see what that improvement could be. Maybe you will see how a slightly different pose could have improved a picture or perhaps how the lighting could have been different. Look at your pictures carefully, and if you have learned anything at all from your course you will probably see other ways that you could have tackled the subject. When you do, write them down, but be brief. At most, an A4 page is all that is necessary.

## The practical submission

City & Guilds reserve a considerable number of marks for good presentation. It is, therefore, worth while taking some trouble with your final presentation. Prints, both colour and black and white, can be submitted – as can slides. With the exception of the colour modules, you can mix black and white and colour. While City & Guilds do not make a specific recommendation, it is felt that students should not mix prints and slides in their submissions. The reason for this is that it is not easy to assess students work when submitted as a mixture of slides and prints. Submit *either* slides *or* prints. One excellent way of presenting your prints is to put them in one of the A4 presentation albums sold by most good stationers. These are bound volumes containing 20 or more transparent sleeves into which prints and written material can easily be inserted. A finished submission using one of these looks good, is inexpensive and is very acceptable for the City & Guilds examination. The workbook need be no more than an exercise book that can be inserted in the back of the album, together with any necessary contact prints or negatives.

Photography is essentially a practical subject. Students aspiring to a City & Guilds 9231 qualification must be prepared to take lots of photographs and to develop a very critical eye when viewing their own pictures and the work of other photographers.

This book will also be helpful to students taking other courses. It covers virtually all the theory requirements for the GCSE examination. GCE 'A' Level students will also find much of the theory useful. In particular they will find the chapter on colour a great help in understanding the complexities of the photographic reproduction of colour. Also, the suggestion in that chapter regarding a simple means of describing how colour works will avoid a large amount of 'commiting to memory', which is always an advantage for students.

Lastly, this book is also for those who are not taking any specific course but would like to improve their photography – or to learn how to take good pictures from scratch.

Two famous photographic pioneers, Hurter and Driffield, once wrote:

> *The production of a perfect picture by means of photography is an art. The production of a technically perfect negative is a science.*

And in a recent editorial in the *British Journal of Photography* this statement appeared:

> *The photographer is yet to be born who has risen to the top of his profession – and stayed there – without a proper understanding of, and an ability to control, the technicalities of the medium.*

These two quotations, perhaps, summarise the philosophy not only of this book but of most of the City & Guilds 9231 modules.

# 1 Picture Composition

At the end of this chapter you should be able to understand what is meant by a good composition, apply the three fundamental guidelines of good composition in both your own and other people's photographs and recognise compositional faults in pictures.

---

## Exercise

Before studying this chapter, you should load your camera and take photographs of a number of familiar subjects. These could include your garden, your home, the local high street, a statue, a portrait of a person outdoors and perhaps a portrait taken indoors. Take plenty of pictures and process the film as soon as possible. Make a careful note of the subjects because you will photograph them again later.

---

One basic definition of composition is: 'The pleasing selection and arrangement of objects within the picture area.' In order to achieve pleasing composition, three things – and three things only – need to be remembered. Everything else fits in almost automatically.

- Your picture needs a theme or message.
- You need to draw attention to those things in your picture that state the message or express the theme.
- You need to keep your picture as simple as possible. Keep those parts of the picture that express the theme or tell the story and eliminate or reduce anything that does not.

Now let us have a closer look at each of these rules of composition.

## Express a theme

When someone else looks at your photograph the idea you had when you took the picture should be clearly understood by that person. The message you want to get across, the theme, can be an obvious one. It can, for example, be just a straightforward subject that you have photographed: a house, a portrait of a girl or a group of children playing by the sea.

These are very obvious themes. They are solid concrete messages. They are very easily understood. However, there are abstract messages you may wish to convey. These can express emotions: fear, anger, sadness, a sense of foreboding are all emotions that can be portrayed pictorially. In a landscape, heavy menacing clouds can give an impression of foreboding or even fear. We are all familiar with how facial expressions and bodily postures give us an impression of how a person is feeling so, if we want to express anger, we can ask our subject to look angry.

It is important to have an idea of what you want to show in your picture, and to use some means of drawing attention to that message, otherwise the viewer may not realise what you had in mind. This brings us to thinking about the second guideline – which is how to emphasise your theme.

## Emphasis

There are very many ways of drawing attention to those parts of your picture that you use to express your theme. The first of these is to arrange your picture so that there is an obvious centre of interest. Try to arrange other parts of the picture area in such a way that they will complement what you have chosen as your centre of interest. Pictures with more than one centre of interest can tend to be confusing (compare Figures 1.1 and 1.2).

If you find, when looking at a picture, that your eye tends to flick backwards and forwards from one part of the picture to the other ask yourself whether there are two centres of interest conflicting with one another. If you have a true centre of interest this should be the area that your eye naturally falls upon when you first look at the picture and to which the eye returns after scanning the rest of the picture area. But it does help to use some means of giving extra

Fig. 1.1 A confusing picture with more than one centre of interest.

Fig. 1.2 A well-composed picture with one centre of interest. The figure on the beach looking at the wreck adds interest and serves to direct the viewer's eye back to the main subject. (Photo: J.B. Wayne.)

emphasis to your centre of interest and there are a number of compositional devices which you can use and which can be most effective. **Framing** is one of these devices.

## Framing

Framing is one of the most effective means of emphasis. A landscape or a building will nearly always gain if you photograph it from under a tree in such a way as to allow the branches of the tree to form a natural frame along the top and/or sides of your picture. Another kind of frame could be a doorway or window; if you take your picture through one of these and allow the edges of that doorway or window to appear in your picture, then the scene can be nicely framed. There are numerous other possibilities – such as the arch of a bridge – all of which can form effective frames drawing attention to your subject. Remember, however, that in general terms the frame is always between the camera and the subject (Figure 1.3).

## Leading lines

Another most effective means of drawing attention to your subject is the use of leading lines. A little river winding along in your photograph can be used to draw attention to the mountains in the background. A line of white posts can be used to draw attention to someone sitting on one of them. The natural lines of the hills in a landscape can be used to bring the eye down to a village or a lake nestling in the foothills. The leading lines of the masts of a ship can

Fig. 1.3 A winter landscape well framed between two trees and hanging branches.

draw attention to the ship itself. Railway lines can draw very striking attention to an approaching train. There are many ways that you can use leading lines to draw attention to your subject and you should keep an eye open for them (Figure 1.4).

## Intersection of thirds

The intersection of thirds in a rectangular picture are very strong points of emphasis. To see how this works, divide your picture into three equal areas horizontally by ruling two lines across, as shown in Figure 1.5, then draw two lines vertically dividing the picture into three equal areas in the vertical plane. The four points where the lines intersect, which have been circled in the figure, are points of very powerful visual attraction. If you place your subject, therefore, at any of these points it will gain substantial emphasis (Figure 1.6). For instance, a landscape or a seascape in which the horizon is in the position of one of the horizontal thirds always looks a great deal better than if the horizon line is right through the middle of the picture.

Fig. 1.4 The figure on the beach here is nicely emphasised by both leading lines and framing.

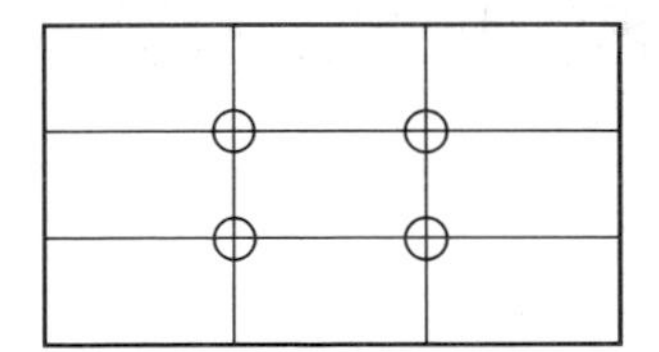

Fig. 1.5 The intersection of thirds.

Fig. 1.6 The dancer in the picture is placed in the top-right-hand position of thirds.

### Tones and colours

Tones and colours can also be used with great effect in drawing attention to your subject. It is a general rule that the eye will always look at the lightest area in a picture. An obvious example is a person in white clothes photographed against a sombre background. You can draw attention to your subject by making it lighter in the picture area than other things. Be careful of light objects, however, because unwanted and unnoticed light objects can cause serious problems (as discussed later).

Bright, saturated colours and colours of the so-called 'warm' variety will pull the eye towards them like a magnet. Saturated reds, yellows and oranges are particularly powerful. The 'cooler' colours and those that are less saturated work in the opposite manner. It is always better, therefore, to use a blue background for a portrait rather than a red one.

### Repetition

Another useful tool of emphasis is repetition. In Figure 1.7 the picture on the artist's canvas and the scene being painted make up a powerful repetitive visual stimulus to draw attention to the subject.

## Rule of simplicity

This third rule, the rule of simplicity, is probably the most important. Many pictures disappoint because they contain numerous features of interest.

Our eyes are very ready to deceive us whenever we look at someone or something. We automatically disregard anything that we are not interested in and concentrate on whatever it is that holds our attention. For instance, if we see someone standing in the street we look at that person and we don't see the car or bicycle in the background, the rubbish bin in the foreground or perhaps a bit of old newspaper lying on the footpath. Nor do we see that lamp-post immediately behind the subject which, in the finished print, will look as if it is growing out of that person's head. Then there is that snapshot of cousin Mabel taken at the bottom of the garden. When

Fig. 1.7 Repetition is used to attract the viewer's attention in this unusual picture.

we looked at her standing there, everything seemed fine and the hedge at the bottom of the garden seemed to be a very attractive background. But when the picture came back from the processor, cousin Mabel was very small and was surrounded by grass, hedge and sky which occupied most of the picture area.

These disappointing situations can easily be avoided. A little thought is all that is needed. Alfred Eisenstaedt, one of the most famous of all of *Life Magazine*'s photographers, says that the first thing he looks at before taking a picture is the background. That is an excellent rule and will save lots of spoiled pictures.

To apply the third guideline, always check carefully the whole of the scene that you are going to photograph to see if you can move in closer or possibly change your viewpoint to cut out any distracting items such as that awkwardly placed lamp-post, a pile of rubbish, too much sky or too much grass.

Those things in no way help the picture. Snapshots are often disappointing simply because the photographer did not move in close enough to the subject. Except in very special cases, a good photograph has only one centre of interest – this follows on naturally from keeping the picture as simple as possible. Look at your pictures and, as we discussed earlier, see if your eye goes to one particular area in the picture and returns to that area again and again. If it does, then you probably have a good picture.

## Exercise

Now you are ready to take pictures of the same subjects you photographed in the first exercise. Go back to exactly the same places, but this time apply the rules of photographic composition to your pictures. Compare carefully both sets of pictures. Which shots do you like best – those taken before you studied this chapter, or those taken after?

## Using the fundamental guidelines

Now that you have studied the fundamental guidelines of good photographic composition you should always apply them whenever you take pictures. Before you press the shutter button ask yourself three questions:

- What is the message or theme I want in my picture?
- What means can I use to emphasise that message?
- Is there anything in my picture that I don't need?

If you apply the guidelines rigorously when taking your pictures, and if you are using the positive/negative technique when making or ordering your enlargements, you really will be delighted by the

**Fig. 1.8** An interesting shot but somewhat confusing as the boat tends to become mixed up with the reflections in the water. (Photo: Keith Hawkins.)

Fig. 1.9 The 'Giant's Chair' in the Forest of Dean is well framed between the trees. However, the fence across the path is a little distracting. A closer viewpoint or perhaps a trim could have eliminated this.

speed with which your composition improves. When applying guideline number three in particular, don't be afraid to cut your prints drastically. Leaving too much in your picture is perhaps the commonest fault of all. Be quite ruthless and cut out anything that does not contribute to the message you want to convey. (See, for example, Figures 1.8–1.10.)

Rules, they say, are meant to be broken and as the above rules are only guidelines, they can be broken for creative effect. Before you

Fig. 1.10 This view at Dedham needs simplification. The swans, ducks and people (with their reflections) on the opposite bank of the river, all compete with each other for the viewer's attention.

break them, however, do make sure you fully understand how they work. If you do, then you will know just how far you need to break them to get the effect you really want.

## Summary

**In this chapter we have shown you how to use the basic rules of good composition to improve your pictures. Get into the habit of applying the guidelines not only of your own pictures but every time you look at a picture in a book, magazine or at an exhibition and then ask yourself this question: 'Could I have made a better picture of that subject by applying the guidelines?' You may be surprised at the answers.**

# 2 Cameras and Lenses

When you have completed this chapter you will understand:

- the construction and working of the main types of camera
- the use of different sizes of film and negative formats in relation to the main types of camera
- the functions of lenses
- 'depth of field' and 'perspective'

Basically all cameras are the same. They consist of a light-tight box. At one end of the box is something that can be used to gather light and project an image of the subject. At the other end of the box is a place for the sensitive material – the film.

The camera itself was invented long before it was possible to record the image. The so-called *camera obscura* was very similar to a modern camera but instead of the film there was a screen upon which you could see the projected image. The *camera obscura* was used extensively by artists who could trace the images formed and produce drawings and silhouettes.

The image-forming device can be a simple pinhole or a lens. In Figure 2.1 we illustrate a simple pinhole camera. Figure 2.2 shows that the image formed in a pinhole camera is upside down. Our diagram shows the path of rays of light through the pinhole. Light

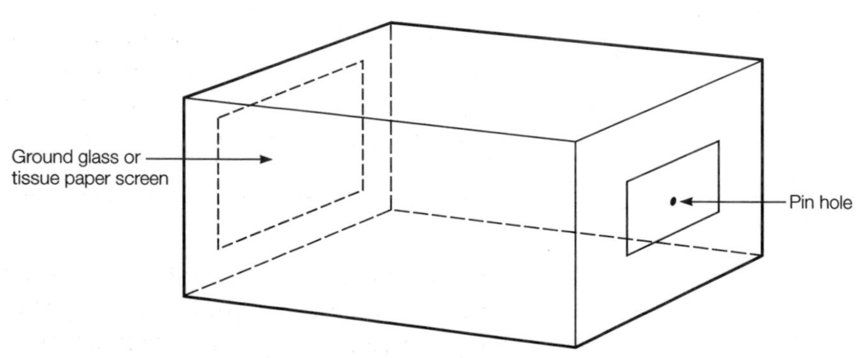


**Fig. 2.1** Pinhole camera.

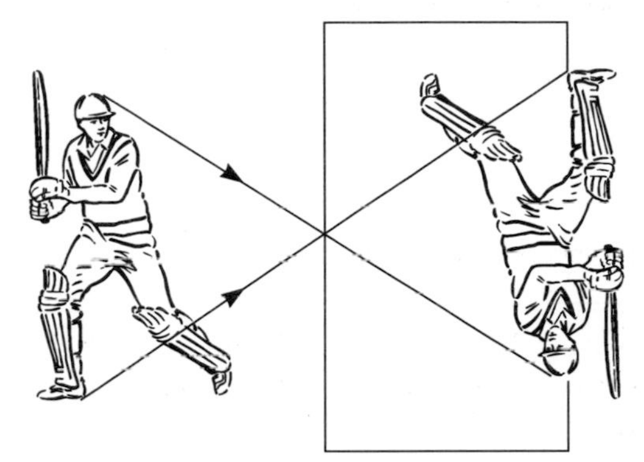

Fig. 2.2 Image formation by a pinhole.

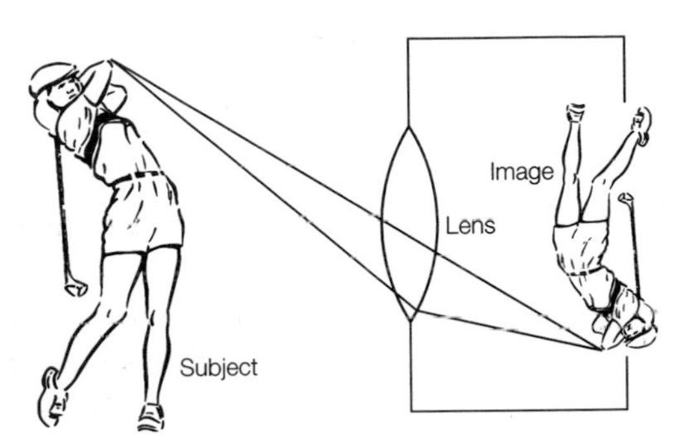


Fig. 2.3 Image formation by a lens.

travels in straight lines, which is why the image is upside down. The disadvantage of a pinhole camera is that the image is very dim. It is possible to make the pinhole larger but the larger it is the more the image becomes indistinct. Even with a very small pinhole the image is still lacking in critical sharpness.

In order to improve sharpness and brightness of the image in a camera a lens is used. If you open the back of your camera you will see that at one end of the light-tight box there is a lens, and at the other end there is a place for the film. Figure 2.3 shows how an image is formed in the camera by its lens. The figure shows a simple lens, such as an ordinary magnifying glass, which can produce images fairly well.

## Exercise

You can illustrate this very easily by the use of a magnifying glass and a piece of white notepaper. Find a place in a room, opposite the window, so that the end of the room is a little darker than anywhere else. If you then hold up the magnifying glass between the window and the paper and move the paper backwards and forwards you will see formed on the paper a reasonably sharp image of the window.

A simple lens like a magnifying glass has indeed been used in cameras and the very simplest box type cameras and some of today's so-called 'disposable' cameras use a simple lens similar to a magnifying glass.

In order to produce a really sharp image, however, more complex lenses are necessary and modern lenses are made up of a number of specially shaped elements composed of specially formulated glasses. The structures of lenses are designed to give the best possible sharpness. It is necessary, too, that light of different wavelengths (colours) are focused in the same plane, and to correct other optical defects that can occur. We shall look at some of these in our discussion of lenses.

In order to obtain a satisfactory photograph it is necessary to get the exposure as nearly correct as possible. Exposure is defined as the **amount** of light reaching the film. We shall discuss exposure in much greater detail in Chapter 5, but now, however, we need to understand that exposure consists of two components:

- the quantity of light reaching the film
- the time that the light falls on the film

Most cameras have means of controlling these two factors. The quantity of light is controlled by the size of the aperture in the lens. This is the hole through which the light passes. Obviously the larger the hole, more light will pass and, conversely, the smaller the hole, less light will pass. As a rough comparison we can see that a lot of water will pass through a large pipe, while much less water will pass through a small one. Some lenses have fixed apertures but most, particularly the advanced types, have a means of changing the aperture. We shall see how this is done later.

The other control is the length of time light is allowed to fall on the film. This is done by a shutter mechanism. In its simplest form the functions of a shutter can simply be a means of uncovering and covering the lens. Indeed, in some older studio cameras this is exactly the procedure that is used. However, with modern cameras, mechanical means are used whereby either a set of blades can be opened and closed in the light path or a moving blind system can be used. Experiments are well advanced for the use of liquid crystals using this principle and working shutter mechanisms have been demonstrated. However, these are still a long way from general introduction.

## Review

**Two of the main controls of a camera are the *iris diaphragm* which controls the quantity of light passing through the lens and**

**the *shutter* which controls the length of time that the light is allowed to pass.**

The third fundamental control of a camera is the means of producing a sharp image. This is called **focusing** and is generally carried out by allowing the whole lens or parts of it to move backwards and forwards in a focusing mount. The nearer the camera is to the subject the further from the film plane is the focusing element of the lens. Simple cameras sometimes have fixed focus lenses. Satisfactory results can be obtained from fixed focus lenses by taking advantage of another property of lens systems – depth of field – something which we shall discuss in detail later. Most cameras, however, have a means of focusing the image.

## Camera types

Cameras are usually classified according to two characteristics. The first of these is the way in which the camera is aimed at the subject. You must know what you are getting on your film and there are several ways of aiming the camera and knowing exactly, or nearly so, what is going to be in your picture. The other characteristic is the way in which lenses are focused. On this basis there are four kinds of camera:

- viewfinder/rangefinder cameras
- twin-lens reflex cameras (TLRs)
- single-lens reflex cameras (SLRs)
- studio, view and technical cameras

### Viewfinder/ rangefinder cameras

Figure 2.4 shows a diagram of a typical viewfinder camera. The viewfinder is a small optical device placed usually on the top of the camera and to one side in relation to the lens and is used to show what will be in the picture. Many simple cameras have this kind of device. Cameras which incorporate an optical rangefinder

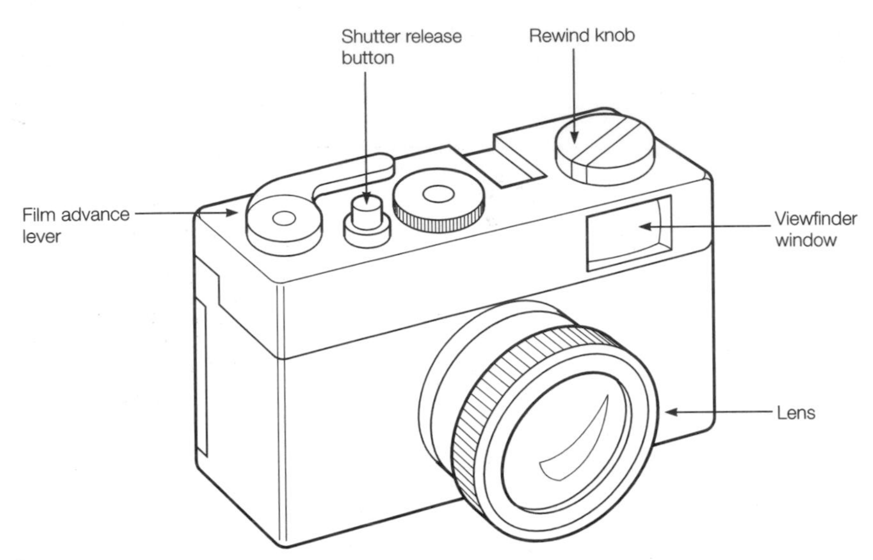


Fig. 2.4 A 35-mm viewfinder camera.

Fig. 2.5 Cut-away view of a viewfinder camera fitted with a rangefinder and facility for interchangeable lenses. (Photo: Leica Camera Ltd.)

sometimes have this device incorporated in the viewfinder, or possibly a small separate window to one side of the viewfinder. The rangefinder mechanism is coupled to the movement of the lens and allows you to focus precisely on your subject. Rangefinders produce two images of the subject which merge together in the eyepiece

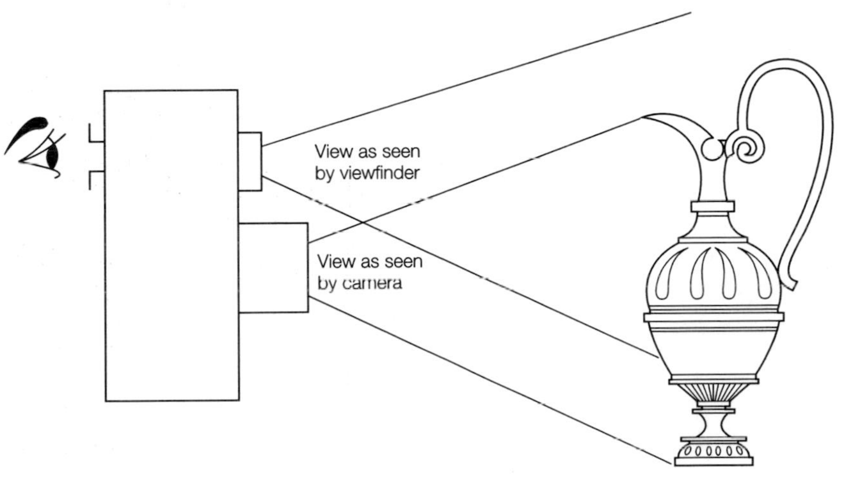


Fig. 2.6 Parallax error.

when sharp focus is achieved. Figure 2.5, shows a cut-away model of the Leica viewfinder camera, which is fitted with a coupled rangefinder.

Most of the modern viewfinder cameras are so-called compacts which have fixed lenses that cannot be changed. The Leica camera is an example of the few, more expensive, precision viewfinder/ rangefinder cameras that feature interchangeable lenses.

Advantages

1. The subject is visible at all times through the viewfinder.
2. The image seen in the viewfinder is bright, which makes the camera easy to use when the light level is low.
3. The shutter usually operates quietly and so does not attract attention to the photographer.

Disadvantages

1. As the image in the viewfinder always looks sharp, it is possible to forget to focus the camera. If your camera is an autofocus type, then this is not a problem for most subjects.
2. Since the viewfinder and taking lens are separated, the image recorded on the film is not exactly the same as the subject seen through the viewfinder. This is called **parallax error**. For most subjects at a reasonable distance from the camera parallax error is negligible and so is not noticed. It does become important, however, when taking close-ups. Figure 2.6 shows why this is so. In some cameras, such as the Leica, the actual frame in the viewfinder moves as you focus in close and this movement will compensate for parallax error.

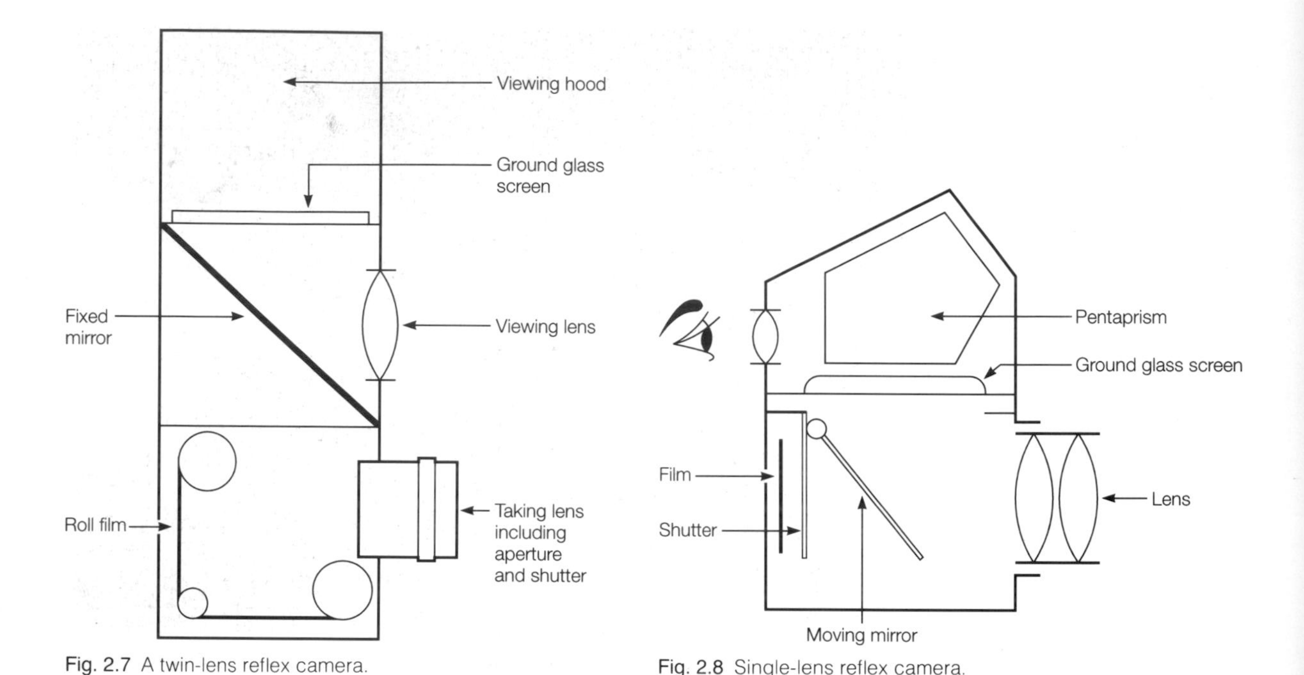


Fig. 2.7 A twin-lens reflex camera.

Fig. 2.8 Single-lens reflex camera.

## Twin-lens reflex cameras (TLRs)

These cameras are really two cameras in one. One camera is mounted on top of the other, as shown in Figure 2.7. The bottom camera is fitted with the taking lens, its aperture control, the shutter and the film. The top camera is fitted with a lens of the same characteristics as the taking lens and projects an image of the subject via a mirror on to a ground-glass screen. Both lenses use the same focusing mechanism.

The ground-glass screen is used both to compose the picture and to focus sharply on the subject. Twin-lens reflex cameras appeared in the 1930s and became very popular for press and fashion work. The Rolleiflex was the pioneer and is still in production. A Japanese model featuring interchangeable lens systems is also available.

### Advantages

1. The subject is visible at all times on the ground-glass screen.
2. The shutter mechanism is as quiet as with viewfinder/rangefinder cameras.
3. The image can be seen on the ground-glass screen the same size as it will appear in the negative and so facilitates composition of

Fig. 2.9 Leica single-lens reflex cameras and a selection of interchangeable lenses for use with them. (Photo: Leica Camera Ltd.)

the subject. At the same time it is possible to focus on the most important part of the subject.

### Disadvantages

1. Because the viewing lens is separate from the taking lens, parallax error occurs, particularly when taking close-ups.
2. Because the image is reflected in a mirror before being projected on the ground-glass screen, it is seen right way up but reversed from right to left. This means that it is very difficult to follow moving subjects. To alleviate this problem, some advanced TRL cameras have a direct viewing device so that the subject can be viewed and composed directly through a framing system. Focusing, however, must still be carried out on the ground-glass screen.

## Single-lens reflex cameras (SLRs)

The fundamental difference between single-lens reflex cameras and viewfinder/rangefinder or twin-lens reflex cameras is that the single-lens reflex type allows you to use the taking lens as a viewfinder.

Figure 2.8 is a diagram of a typical single-lens reflex camera. As with the twin-lens reflex, light entering the lens is reflected by a mirror on to a ground-glass screen. The mirror is on a pivot so that immediately before the picture is taken the mirror moves up out of the light path, the shutter opens and the image is formed on the film surface.

The apparatus on the top of the camera is an optical device called a **pentaprism** which not only allows the photographer to view the subject at eye level but also shows the image on the ground-glass screen right way up and reversed left to right so that the orientation of the subject is returned to its normal state. After the picture has been taken the mirror flips down again and the camera is ready for the next exposure.

A Leica single-lens reflex camera and its range of available lenses are shown in Figure 2.9.

### Review

**To summarise, the operation of a single-lens reflex follows this sequence when the shutter button is depressed:**

- **the mirror swings upwards**
- **the shutter opens**
- **the shutter closes**
- **the mirror swings down again**

Advantages

1. The photographer sees in the viewfinder exactly what will be on the film, there is no parallax error.
2. Focusing on the ground-glass screen guarantees that the picture will be in focus on the film.
3. It is possible to use a very wide range of interchangeable lenses, including zoom lenses, without making complicated changes to the viewfinder because whatever the lens sees, and subsequently puts on the film, can be seen in the viewfinder.
4. It is easy to see the effect on the picture of special-effects attachments and filters, such as polarising filters, star filters, prism-effect filters and distorting surfaces.

Disadvantages

1. When the light intensity is low, viewing and focusing can become difficult.
2. The viewfinder blacks out at the time the picture is taken, and the view cannot be seen until the mirror flips down again.
3. There is a short delay between pressing the shutter button and the shutter opening. This is the time taken for the mirror to flip out of the way. The time taken for this to happen is in the region of 1/30 of a second.
4. The action of the mirror in some cameras is quite noisy and can draw attention to the photographer. In some churches the officiator will not allow single-lens reflex cameras to be used during services or weddings.

## Studio, view and technical cameras

This family of cameras includes monorail and field cameras. A variant, but close relative, is the 5 in. × 4 in. press cameras of earlier years, such as the famous Speed Graphic. A typical view camera can be seen in Figure 2.10.

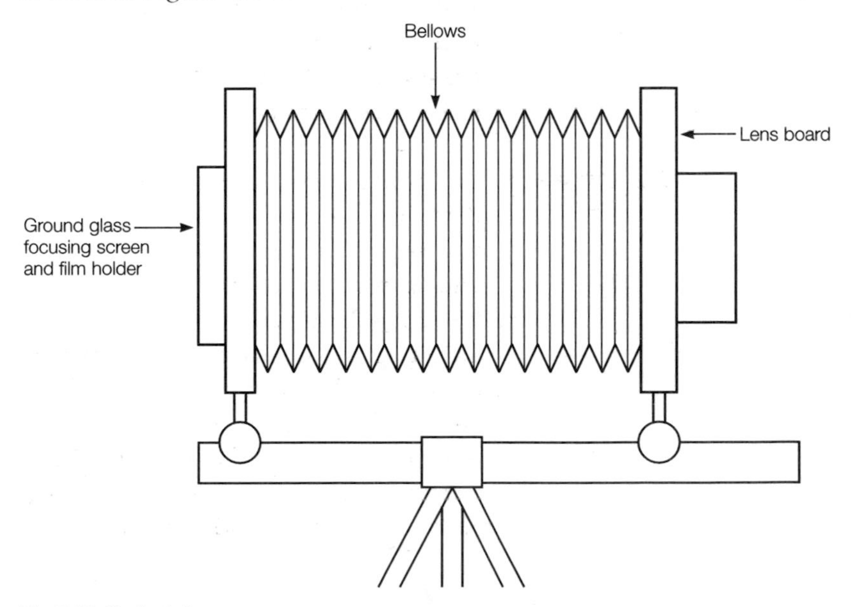


**Fig. 2.10** Typical view camera.

As you will see, there are two panels connected by a bellows. On one panel is the lens and shutter, and on the other panel there is a ground-glass screen. This can be quickly and easily replaced by a holder containing the film. In the past the holders were made to take glass plates that had been coated with photographic emulsion, but sheets of film are now used. There are also available roll film holders for this kind of camera as well as special backs capable of taking Polaroid films.

In using one of these cameras the shutter is opened and the lens panel is moved backwards and forwards while the image on the ground-glass screen is studied. When the composition is right and the image sharp the shutter is closed and the ground-glass screen is replaced by the film holder – called a dark slide. The light-tight sheath is removed from the film holder, the shutter is fired and the exposure made. The sheath is returned to the film holder, which is removed from the camera to await development of the film.

Advantages

1. The large film sizes that can be used in view cameras are capable of producing very high quality photographs more easily than with small formats.
2. There are no parallax errors (except in the case of press cameras).
3. The relative angles of the film plane and the lens plane can be changed. Such movements enable the photographer to change the image, by altering the area of the subject which is in focus and to change perspective. The perspective control aspect can be used to make sure that in the print a tall building appears with parallel sides instead of converging sides.

Disadvantages

1. View cameras can be very heavy and cumbersome.
2. View cameras are slow to use, there being a lengthy delay between setting up the picture, focusing and finally putting in the film holder and taking the picture.
3. They need to be on a sturdy tripod or other firm camera support.
4. They are not suitable for action photography.

Press camera

The notable exception, of course, is the press camera. These cameras have many of the features of a view camera but in addition have a viewfinder/rangefinder system. This is mounted on the backboard or standard. This modification means that the camera can be used relatively quickly and can be hand-held. Parallax error, however, is very severe in these cameras because of the considerable distance by which the viewfinder and taking lens are separated.

## Picture format and film types

Picture format describes the shape and size of the negative produced by a camera. Film sizes such as 110 or disc are used in snapshot cameras. Negatives produced by these cameras can produce fair enlargements up to about 5 × 7 in. Very close in size to the 110 films are those produced by the sub-miniature cameras, such as the famous Minox 'spy' cameras. These sub-miniature films and cameras are capable of considerably better results than most 110 or disc cameras but the very small size of the negative makes enlarging a difficult process and it is rare to be able to produce a really good print larger than 8 × 10 in.

The smallest practical format is the 24 × 36-mm negative which most 35-mm cameras produce on standard 35-mm film. Larger sized formats are produced on roll film, usually designated either 120 or 220. Larger sizes are produced on sheet film. In earlier times emulsions were coated on glass plates and a few special purpose glass plates are still manufactured.

The sizes of negatives produced on the most common formats are compared in Figure 2.11. For special purposes, larger sheet films are available, 8 × 10 in. being quite common.

35-mm film

The majority of viewfinder and single-lens reflex cameras use 35-mm film. This film is supplied in cassettes in lengths that will give 12, 20, 24 or 36 exposures. Longer lengths in bulk film packages are also available. 35-mm film originated as motion picture film and

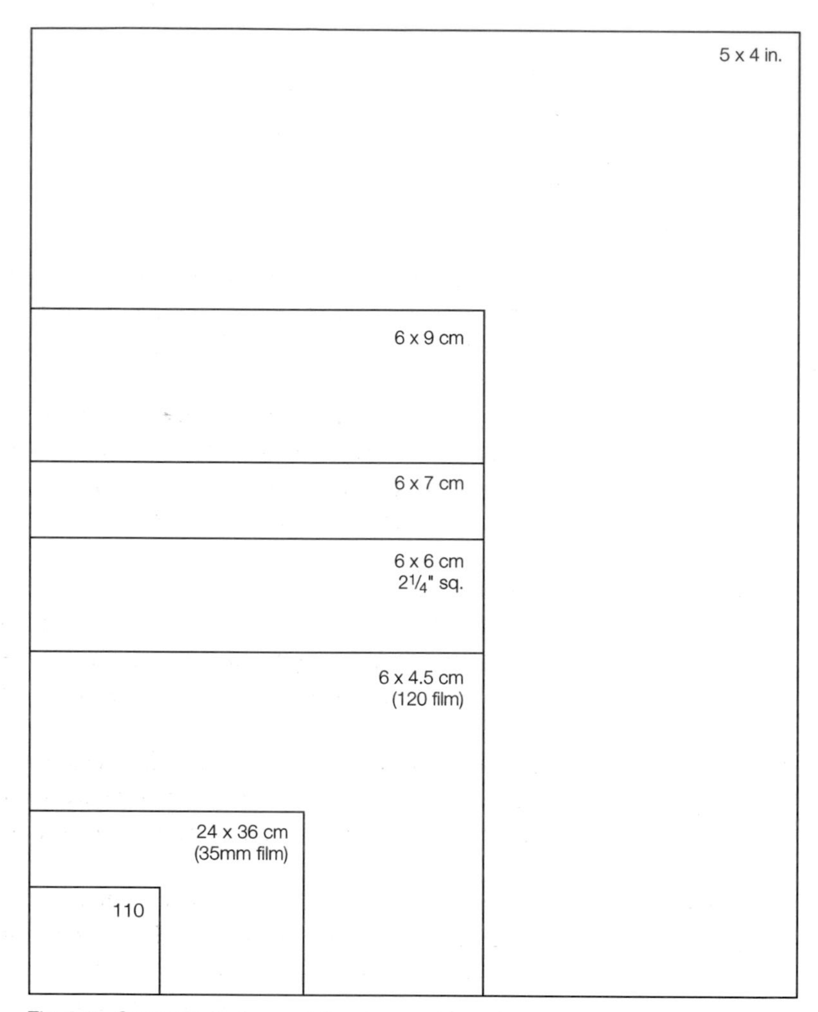


Fig. 2.11 Comparison of current film sizes and formats.

that is why it has perforated edges. The first 35-mm cameras were designed to use this film and to take advantage of the perforations in the film transport mechanism. The first successful 35-mm camera was the Leica.

## 120 and 220 film

120 and 220 films are supplied rolled on to a spool and are often called **roll films**. Both are of the same width but 220 film is twice as long as 120. 120 film is supported by a roll of backing paper but 220 film has the backing paper just at the beginning and ends. Some roll film cameras will not take 220 film and at present it can be difficult to obtain.

The picture format produced on 120 and 220 film depends on the camera. There are very many different formats available, some of them are as follows:

- 6 × 4.5 cm. This is produced by some single-lens reflex cameras and gives fifteen negatives on a 120 film roll.
- 6 × 6 cm (2¼ in. square). This is produced by most twin-lens reflex cameras, notably the Hasselblad. This format gives twelve negatives per 120 film.
- 6 × 7 cm and 6 × 9 cm. These formats can be produced by certain of the large single-lens reflex cameras and some older roll film folding cameras. They are also produced by the roll film backs available for use on view and technical cameras.

## Specialist roll films

There are some special purpose films such as rolls of varying lengths and 70 mm wide; these are used in specialist cameras in, for example, the department store portrait business.

## Instant films

Polaroid were the pioneers of so called 'instant' photography. Rapid processing with prints produced in a few minutes had long been known and practised, especially by street photographers. However, Polaroid produced a technique whereby the picture could be taken and, by a most ingenious mechanical and chemical system, the film could be processed in the camera to produce a negative and a peel-off print produced by chemical image transfer. This took place in a minute or less. Improvements in the basic technique have been made over the years and other manufacturers have marketed instant films. The introduction of colour made the process more popular and the technology behind the polaroid colour process is one of the marvels of modern chemical technology. It is beyond the scope of this book to discuss instant photography in any detail. Polaroid photography is enormously useful to the professional photographer because it provides a means of instantly checking lighting set-ups and compositional details of complicated sets. It also finds wide application in the fields of passport and identification photography.

A few years ago Polaroid introduced instant 8-mm cine photography. A movie camera could expose a length of film. It would then be passed through a special processor/viewer and could be viewed within a few minutes. The system was marketed too late to be a success because it could not compete with the rise of video tape and video cameras. An off-shoot, Polaroid instant 35-mm film, however, remains and has useful applications, especially in the quick preparation of slides for lecture purposes. Polaroid 35-mm film can be exposed in any 35-mm camera. After exposure it is processed in a special Polaroid 35-mm processing apparatus. The finished film can be viewed only a few minutes after the last exposure has been taken.

## Other means of image production

Until now we have discussed only the formation of an image taking advantage of the sensitivity of silver salts to light. That is the silver-based image. A new process, digital photography, has appeared in recent years. Here electronic means are used to capture the image and to make prints. As with ordinary photography, a camera is used and the image is converted to a video signal and stored on tape or disc. The stored image is later digitised and displayed on a television screen or equipment used to make a conventional print. The Kodak CD (compact disc) system is an example. Here existing images made on convential photographic materials are scanned, digitised and transferred to disc for later electronic display or conversion to a conventional print.

At present, still video methods – although improving constantly – have not reached the resolution or quality standards achievable with silver techniques. One technique which is achieving excellent results is the digital conversion of silver images and their subsequent manipulation. Changes to photographs can be made which are virtually undetectable, bringing a whole new dimension to the old myth 'the camera never lies'.

## Camera lenses

Camera lenses have two functions:

- to collect light rays from the subject
- to focus those rays of light on the film so as to produce a sharp image

As we saw earlier, a simple magnifying glass will produce an image. However, for most photographic purposes a higher quality image is required. This can only be obtained from lenses made by putting together a number of different-shaped glass elements. Such lenses are known as **compound lenses**. The use of a number of elements enables the lens designer to correct optical faults inherent in a simple lens.

Figure 2.12 shows a cut-away section of a modern Leica lens. The best quality lenses have three or more elements. Three-element lenses are widely used but, for the finest results, four or more elements are essential.

Fig. 2.12 Cut-away view of a typical modern lens. (Photo: Leica Camera Ltd.)

## Focusing the lens

As we saw in our simple experiment with a magnifying glass, an image of a window was formed on the paper when we held the magnifying glass at a certain distance from the paper. If we moved the glass further from or nearer to the paper then the image became less sharp. To obtain a sharp image of our subject on the film it is necessary for us to be able to change the distance of the lens from the film. As we get nearer the subject, it is necessary to increase the distance between the lens and the film.

Bearing in mind these fundamental points, let us look at the different kinds of cameras and the way they focus the image.

### Fixed focus cameras

The simplest cameras, including the new disposable cameras and the older box cameras, have fixed focus lenses and there are no facilities for focusing. Occasionally a so-called 'close-up setting' for portraits is provided. This is usually in the form of a simple supplementary lens which can be moved in front of the taking lens. Fixed focus cameras are constructed in such a way that they produce reasonably good pictures of everything between a distance of about 5 feet and the far horizon. Disappointing, out-of-focus pictures with these cameras always result if the photographer moves too close to the subject.

### Variable focus cameras and lenses

Variable focus cameras and lenses are constructed so that the lens or an element of it can be moved in and out to enable the subject to be focused accurately on the film plane. In some cameras the lens is simply set against a distance scale. In others, such as coupled rangefinder cameras, the built-in rangefinder, which is linked to the lens movement, is used to focus accurately. In the single-lens reflex camera you can see in the viewfinder how sharply the subject is focused on the ground glass and make the necessary adjustments to the focusing ring on the lens.

### Automatic focusing lenses

There are now available a wide range of cameras and lenses which use electronic sensor and sophisticated mechanisms to focus lenses automatically on a selected subject. There is no longer any need to focus the lens. You just point the camera at your selected subject, press the shutter button, and the camera will do the rest. Some cameras can even be set to take the picture automatically when the subject is in optimum focus. While these facilities can be very convenient, remember that there are disadvantages in automation, as we shall discuss later. There are a number of different mechanisms for auto focus. Some emit sound waves (inaudible to the human ear) which bounce off the subject and reflect back to a receiver on the camera. This is, of course, based on the sonar technique. Some emit beams of infra-red rays, the reflections of which are detected by the camera. Others use image contrast detectors to estimate optimum sharpness conditions at the film plane. The accuracy of these systems vary and the exact area focused on is usually indicted in the viewfinder. Most rely on a reasonable depth of field for their results and very few have sufficient accuracy to focus on, say, the eye nearest the camera in a close-up portrait taken at wide aperture. For general photography, however, they are a most useful tool for the photographer.

## Close-up focusing

Most lenses will not focus on subjects closer than between 2.5 and 3.5 ft. Closer focusing can be carried out in three ways:

1. You can use close-up supplementary lenses. These are used on the front of the lens like a filter. They are positive magnifying lenses.
2. You can move the lens even further out from the camera than normal. You can do this by placing extension tubes, rings or bellows between the lens and the camera body.
3. There are some lenses which are especially constructed to enable you to move in close without the need for supplementary lenses or extension tubes. These are called **macro lenses**. Like zoom lenses, they have a set of elements that can be moved in relation to other elements in the lens to make close focusing possible. Some are able to focus so closely that it is possible to focus accurately on a small insect sitting on the front lens element!

While such lenses can be used for general subjects, they are usually best in the close-up mode and are very useful for photographing small objects such as flowers and insects.

### Review

**There are three main types of camera/lens systems. Fixed focus lenses give a reasonably sharp image over a wide range of distances, usually about 5 ft to infinity. Manual focus lenses enable the user to focus the camera directly. Distance can be set on a scale or a rangefinder system can be provided. Reflex cameras enable focusing to be judged on a screen. Automatic focus cameras use sophisticated electronic systems to focus the lens on the subject.**

## Types of lens

Lenses are often grouped together under four headings. These are:

- normal lenses
- telephoto lenses
- wide-angle lenses
- zoom lenses

### Normal lenses

The so-called 'normal' lens have an angle of view similar to the angle of vision of our eyes. They cover a scene approximately as we would see it with the naked eye. The focal length of a normal lens varies according to the format used. With 35-mm film used in a camera producing a negative of the standard format, 24 × 36 mm, a focal length of 50 mm is generally said to be 'normal'. With 120 roll film in a camera producing negatives 6 × 6 cm, a focal length of 75–85 mm is also regarded as normal.

Recently the whole concept of 'normal' lenses has been called into question and some controversy has arisen. However, as a rough guide, the focal length of a lens which has been considered up to the present as being 'normal' is roughly equal to the length of the diagonal line drawn in the rectangle of the negative format. The diagonal of a 35-mm standard negative is slightly less than 50 mm.

## Telephoto lenses

Telephoto lenses have focal lengths that are longer than normal lenses and wide-angle lenses have shorter focal lengths than normal. For 35-mm cameras, telephoto lenses might have focal lengths of 90, 135, 200, 500 and 1000 mm, or even longer.

## Wide angle lenses

Wide-angle lenses have focal lengths for 35-mm cameras starting at around 35, 28 and 20 mm and sometimes even shorter. A special variant of the wide-angle lens is the so-called 'fish-eye'. Such lenses, giving a circular image, cover an extremely wide angle, sometimes well in excess of 180 degrees, but there is considerable distortion of the image. Such lenses are for specialist applications.

## Zoom lenses

The lenses we have discussed so far have fixed focal lengths. However, there are available a very wide range of lenses with variable focal lengths. Each one can cover the focal length of a considerable number of fixed focus lenses. The advantages of zoom lenses are that instead of changing the lens when you wish to change the focal length, a simple adjustment of a ring on the lens is all that is necessary. Further, you can compose your pictures in the viewfinder without changing the position of the camera in relation to the subject. Zoom lenses are produced in a variety of focal lengths for 35-mm cameras, covering typically wide-angle to standard focal lengths, wide-angle to medium telephoto, standard to longer telephoto and medium telephoto to long telephoto. More recently zoom lenses have appeared which cover a remarkably wide range from wide-angle to long telephoto.

One criticism of zoom lenses had been that they are not of such a high optical quality as fixed focal length lenses and are, therefore, not capable of producing such high-quality pictures. Recent zoom lenses, however, are capable of excellent quality results, and for normal work give a performance indistinguishable from fixed focal length lenses. Their main disadvantage, however, is that usually the maximum aperture is less than fixed focal length lenses and so they let through less light.

### Tele-converters

Tele-converters (sometimes called tele-extenders) are small optical units which act as converters. They can be fitted between your lens and the camera body and act to increase the focal length of your lens. There are 2× converters, 3× converters and some of even higher power. Good quality converters can sometimes be very useful, but they reduce the amount of light, and exposure compensation is therefore necessary. If your camera uses a through-the-lens means of measuring exposure, this will automatically take into account the effect of the converter. If, however, external means are used to measure exposure, then an appropriate correction must be made to your exposure settings. Cheap converters are not advised because their definition can be very poor.

## Lens properties

There are two properties of a lens which are of prime importance in determining how your pictures will look. These are:

- focal length
- lens speed

### Focal length

Lenses are always described first of all by their focal length. The focal length of a lens is defined as the distance between the optical centre of a lens and the image formed by it when that lens is focused on a subject at infinity. In photographic terms infinity, represented by the symbol ∞, means objects at a considerable distance away.

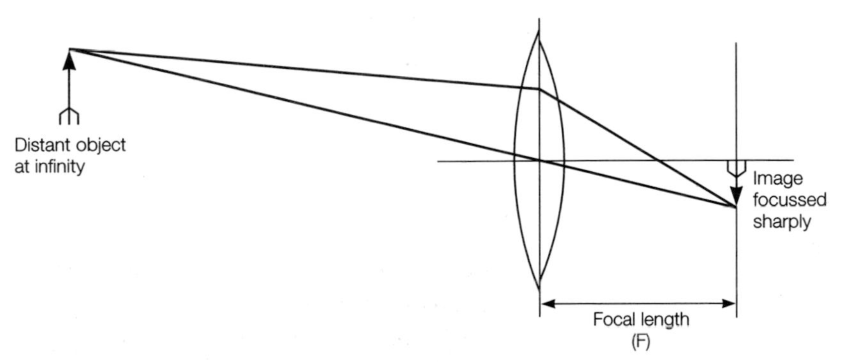


Fig. 2.13 The focal length of a lens.

The horizon is an example. Or, in practice, anything 1000 yards or more from the camera can be considered to be at infinity. Figure 2.13 illustrates the concept of focal length of a lens.

The focal length of a lens directly determines three other aspects of our pictures. These are:

- the size of the subject on the film
- the angle of view
- the relative size of various objects in the scene – this is sometimes referred to as the **perspective** of the scene

#### The size of the subject on the film

In Figures 2.14–2.19 we see a scene photographed from the same position with lenses of different focal lengths. As the focal length of the lens increases, the size of the image of a given object also increases. For example, if we double the focal length then, other things being equal, we will double the linear dimensions of a given image.

#### The angle of view

If you study the photographs again, it can be seen that as the focal length increases, the area of the scene which appears in the picture decreases, so we have the general rules that the longer the focal length of the lens, the smaller the angle of view and the shorter the focal length of the lens, the greater the angle of view. The angle of view of various focal length lenses is illustrated in Figure 2.20.

#### Perspective

Perspective in photographs refers to the relative size of different objects at different distances from the camera. If the scene looks natural, with the various objects in the size relationships that we expect to see when looking with our eyes at a scene, then the perspective looks natural to us. When objects look unnaturally large

Fig. 2.14 20-mm lens.

Fig. 2.15 28-mm lens.

Fig. 2.16 50-mm lens.

Fig. 2.17 135-mm lens.

Fig. 2.18 200-mm lens.

Fig. 2.19 400-mm lens.

or unnaturally small, then the effect can be disturbing. We are all familiar with unnatural perspective in photographs such as the kind of joke picture in which a person's feet look enormous in the foreground and there is a very small head in the distance. Perspective in photographs is governed entirely by the distance of the subject

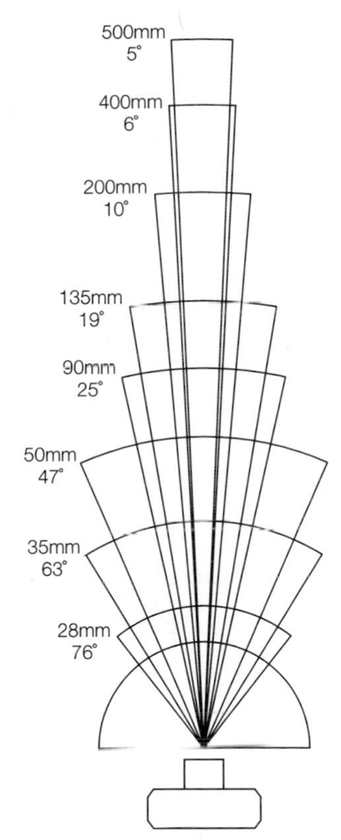


Fig. 2.20 Angle of view and focal length for lenses of varying focal lengths suitable for 35-mm cameras.

Fig. 2.21 Perspective distortion produced by a 20-mm focal length lens being too close to the subject. The picture shows a second degree black belt Aikidoka making a strike. Notice how large the fist nearest the camera appears in relation to the other hand.

from the lens. It is not affected by the focal length of the lens.

Perspective is used by the eye to estimate distances and it gives a feeling of depth and distance in a photograph. As mentioned previously, if the perspective is markedly different from what we expect to see in a natural scene, then unusual perspective can be disturbing. The effect in a photograph is called **perspective distortion** (Figure 2.21).

Fig. 2.22 Linear distortion produced by photographing buildings with a very wide-angle lens.

Because short focal length lenses have a wide angle of view, objects close to wide-angle lenses can be shown very large while objects only a short distance away appear small in the print. This effect can be useful in drawing attention to subjects but if used in taking a portrait can produce a most unflattering effect. A point to remember is that perspective distortion is produced by having the lens *too close* to the subject, regardless of the focal length of that lens.

Taking pictures of buildings with wide-angle lenses can also result in a kind of perspective distortion known as **linear distortion**. If, when photographing a building, we use a wide-angle lens and tip the camera upwards, then in the resulting picture the sides of the building will seem to converge rapidly, as in Figure 2.22.

Actually when we look up at a building our eyes see precisely the same kind of thing – that is, the verticals converge on the retina of our eye in just the same way as they do in the photograph. However, what we see is really a combination of our eye (corresponding to the camera) and our brain. When we look up at a building our eye sees the converging verticals but our brain corrects those verticals for us. It does not do this when we look at a photograph of a building. Therefore, a photograph of a building with converging verticals looks unnatural. Of course for photographic effects we may well wish to produce pictures with converging verticals. If we want to avoid them, however, we must not tilt the camera upwards but make sure that we take the picture from such a viewpoint that the camera can be square on to the sides of the building.

**Perspective distortion by telephoto lenses**

Another kind of perspective distortion is produced when we take a photograph with a very long focal length lens. These lenses have a narrow angle of view, and objects that are some distance from the camera can appear very close to other objects nearby. They can, in fact, appear unnaturally close. This gives the typical bunched-up effect that we see sometimes of buildings or other objects when taken with a long focus lens from a long distance. Portraits taken with lenses of focal lengths greater than 135 mm on 35-mm film can begin to produce 'squashed' facial features.

**Lens speed**

The larger the amount of light that a lens will let through, the shorter the time necessary for the shutter to be open to get correct exposure. The speed of a lens is the way we describe how much light will pass. A so-called 'fast' lens will let more light pass than a 'slow' lens.

Whether a lens is fast or slow depends on the maximum aperture of that lens. We can also control the amount of light passing by changing the size of the aperture of the lens.

## The f/numbers

The size of the aperture of a lens is described by a series of f/numbers. These are sometimes described as 'stops'. The bigger the aperture through which the light passes – and so the greater the amount of light – the smaller the f/number. If you look at a typical lens, as shown in Figure 2.23, you will see that the aperture is marked with a series of numbers. These could be 2, 2.8, 4, 5.6, 8, 11, 16, 22. The smallest number on the setting ring is the largest aperture at which that lens is capable of being set. In the case we

Fig. 2.23 Aperture and distance scales engraved on the mount of a Leica lens. (Photo: Leica Camera Ltd.)

have just quoted, f/2 would be the largest aperture and the smallest would be f/22 for that particular lens.

Table 2.1

| Aperture | Amount of light |
|---|---|
| f/2 | 128 |
| f/2.8 | 64 |
| f/4 | 32 |
| f/5.6 | 16 |
| f/8 | 8 |
| f/11 | 4 |
| f/16 | 2 |
| f/22 | 1 |

The f/numbers are caclulated by dividing the diameter of the opening of the lens into the focal length. Strictly speaking it is the effective size of the opening, which is not quite the same as the actual size. If you have a lens set at f/2 and the focal length is 50 mm, the size of the effective aperture would be 25 mm, i.e. 50/25. Similarly, if a 50-mm lens is set at f/8, the size of the aperture would be 6.25 mm. All lenses which are set to the same f/number let through the same amount of light whatever the maximum aperture of the lens and whatever its focal length. If this were not so, comparative exposures would not be possible.

As we saw, the series of f/numbers marked on a lens could be 2, 2.8, 4, 5.6, 8, 11, 16, 22. These numbers have been chosen so that changing the aperture from one number to the next results in either doubling or halving the amount of light let through the lens. If, for example, we change the aperture from f/5.6 to f/8, we halve the amount of light. Conversely, if we open the lens aperture from 5.6 to 4, we double the amount of light. Table 2.1 sets out these relationships in a little more detail.

The aperture of a lens, therefore, controls the amount of light passing through it. Closing down that aperture reduces the amount of light flowing, just as closing down a tap will reduce the amount of water flowing. The term 'stop', which is often used to describe apertures, comes from the past when the apertures were controlled by a sliding disc in which holes of various sizes were drilled. These were called Waterhouse Stops, and the description 'stops' has survived although most apertures are now controlled by an iris diaphragm.

The size of the aperture and the shutter speed work together to produce the appropriate exposure for the film. However, the size of the aperture has another effect on the final picture. It influences the depth of field. Just how these factors dovetail together will be discussed in the following chapters.

> Note that the aperture series doubles or halves depending on which way you turn the aperture ring. Opening up one stop means doubling the amount of light passing through the lens; closing down by one stop means letting in half the amount of light.

---

## Exercise

Write out the aperture series on the lens of your camera. Choose any aperture in the middle of the range and work out what apertures will let through half, quarter and one-eighth of the amount of your chosen aperture.

Choose another aperture and then work out which apertures will let through double, 4 times, 8 times and 16 times the amount of light of your chosen aperture.

---

## Summary

**In this Chapter we have described the construction and working of the four main types of camera. Picture formats and film types were discussed. The main characteristics and operation of various types of lenses have been described together with manual and automatic focusing techniques. Angle of view and perspective has been explained as well as methods of close-up photography. Aperture systems were described and the f/number series explained.**

---

# 3 Using your Camera

When you have finished this chapter, you will understand the functions of the three basic controls of a camera and how these can be used to produce the kind of picture you want.

Today the variety of cameras available is huge. There is a greater and greater tendency towards automation of the key functions such as exposure determination and focusing. Some cameras can be set to manual mode – if you have one of these, then you should set the camera to be used manually in order to gain an understanding of how the settings actually work. Other cameras have no manual mode – and if you have one of these we suggest you buy a simple manual-only camera and exposure meter to enable you to understand fully the fundamentals of exposure and focusing. Good manual-only cameras, such as Prakticas, can be bought second hand, and very cheaply, at many good dealers and you are advised to consider buying or borrowing one for a time until you have really mastered the fundamentals. A thorough understanding of camera operations is essential if you want to become a really good photographer.

## Basic camera controls

**Focusing**, which is usually carried out by turning a ring or knob on the lens, allows you to control what will be the point of maximum sharpness in your picture. **Shutter speed** and **aperture** controls determine the amount of light that reaches the film. They are used together because changing one will necessitate a change in the other. They also have their own influences on how the photographs will look. Shutter speed is usually adjusted using a control on the top of the camera. The aperture control is usually a ring on the lens.

### Shutter speed

Shutter speeds are measured in fractions of a second. The markings on your shutter speed dial could look like this:

| 1000 | 500 | 250 | 125 | 60 | 30 | 15 | 8 | 4 | 2 | 1 |
|---|---|---|---|---|---|---|---|---|---|---|

It cannot be stressed too strongly how vitally important it is for you to know how to use your camera. You should be completely familiar with every aspect of its use.

Your camera's instruction book should be your bible. If you do not have an instruction book for your camera then you should try to obtain one. You could write to your camera agents in this country or to the manufacturers. Any good photographic store will give you the appropriate addresses. If your camera is an older one, you can often obtain copies of instruction books from Oldtimer Cameras Ltd, PO Box 28, Elstree, Herts, WD6 4SY, telephone 0181-953-5479.

There are also a series of manuals describing the use of many different makes and models of camera in very great detail. In some cases these manuals can be even more helpful than the original instruction books. Such manuals can often be found in your local library or the library will obtain a copy for you through the inter-library loan scheme.

It is specially important to have an instruction book if your camera is one of the new electronically operated models. The basic camera controls are the same but the methods of changing the setting of these can vary considerably and can be quite complex. Without knowing the correct procedures of setting the camera controls, it can be very difficult to use such cameras.

**An instruction book should be regarded as the most essential piece of equipment for any photographer.**

These are all fractions of a second. For example: 250 means 1/250 of a second (1/250 s); 2 would mean half a second (0.5 s); while 1 – often the slowest setting on a camera – will be 1 s. You may also find other settings on your shutter speed dial: B, for instance, stands for brief time or 'bulb'. ('Bulb' because, in days gone by, studio cameras had pneumatic shutter releases which were operated by pressing a bulb at the end of a tube. Usually they would remain open as long as the bulb was pressed.) If you press the shutter button with the dial set to B, the shutter will remain opened while the shutter button is depressed and will close when the button is released. With the T setting the shutter will open when you press the shutter release button and will remain opened until you press it again.

Shutter speed is important in controlling the sharpness of your picture. Too slow a shutter speed can cause blurring from either movement of the camera or subject during exposure. Camera shake is in fact one of the most common causes of disappointing pictures. It is caused by using a shutter speed that is too slow for holding the camera in your hand when taking a picture, or it can be caused by a sudden jab at the shutter button.

A picture spoiled by camera shake usually looks unsharp all over. If you look carefully, you can sometimes see fine lines which should be sharp showing double images. For example, in a portrait the ends of the subject's hairs look double. Or in a landscape, fine branches of trees or fence posts at a distance appear double.

To reduce camera shake it is necessary to reduce the movement of the image on the film while the exposure is being made. This can be done by using a faster shutter speed and/or by steadying the camera to reduce its movement.

The slowest shutter speed that can be safely used when taking photographs with the camera in your hand depends upon:

- the type of camera you have
- the focal length of your lens
- the size of the print you will want from your picture
- how you stand and how you hold your camera when taking a photograph
- your own ability to hold the camera steady

Some people have very steady hands indeed and can take satisfactorily sharp pictures at exposures of half a second or so, while others have difficulty even at 1/125 or 1/250 s. On average, people find that about 1/60 s works well but shutter speeds slower than this can result in camera shake.

In general terms the longer the focal length of your lens, the larger is the image of your subject on the negative. Wide-angle lenses produce smaller images and so slower shutter speeds can safely be used. A useful practical guideline first put forward by Andy Marino, Dean of the New York Institute of Photography, is to take the focal length of the lens you are using in millimetres and convert that to fractions of a second. This figure is then the slowest safe shutter speed for hand-held photography with that particular lens. Therefore, if we have a 50-mm lens, the slowest safe shutter speed is 1/50 s. A 200-mm lens would be 1/200 s, and so on.

Holding your camera properly and using commonsense ways and means of both steadying it and yourself can help to reduce the dangers of camera shake.

> [illegible] way of holding your camera securely. You [illegible]. These include tucking your elbows into your [illegible] hands. With eye-level viewfinder cameras you can press your camera firmly against your forehead (if you do not wear glasses). In the standing position keep your legs straight with both feet flat on the ground. Sometimes it is possible to lean against a wall, or rest your elbows on a convenient surface. Sometimes it can be useful to lie down with your elbows on the ground as an additional camera support. It can be useful to rest the camera on the back of a chair or press it against a wall or a sturdy upright post. A beanbag, or even your camera bag, can sometimes provide a firm support or you can use a tripod or monopod. For slow speeds or time exposures tripods are really excellent. When you buy a tripod, make sure it is reasonably heavy and sturdy. Many small lightweight tripods available today are a waste of money because they simply do not give a firm support to the camera. Use a cable release for exposures longer than 1 second. If there is no provision on your camera for a cable release, you can use the delayed action control for slow shutter speeds, but these will seldom work on B or T settings.

### Movement of the subject

Blur due to the movement of the subject is caused by movement of the image while the exposure is taking place. While camera shake results in the whole image being unsharp, movement of the subject results in the subject being blurred while everything else in the picture is sharp. Blurring due to subject movement can be cured by using a faster shutter speed. The actual shutter speeds required to stop motion depends on how far you are from the subject, the speed of the subject and the direction of its movement relative to the camera. The focal length of your lens is also important. The fastest shutter speeds are necessary when you are close to the subject, it is moving fast and it is moving directly across the camera's field of view.

A car travelling at only 20 miles an hour passing directly in front of the camera may need a shutter speed of 1/500 s or 1/1000 s to freeze its motion. However, if the car is coming directly towards you, then 1/125 s or 1/250 s might be fast enough. If the subject is moving at 45 degrees or so to the lens axis so that the view is partially side on, interesting results can be obtained. Such subjects

Fig. 3.1 Use of a slow shutter speed (1/15 s) has blurred the passing bicycle and given a good impression of movement. (Photo: Keith Hawkins.)

need shutter speeds somewhere between those for head-on or full-side view photographs. Good shots of moving trains can be obtained using this technique and moderately slow shutter speeds are possible.

Usually, subjects moving straight across the field of view require shutter speeds about four times faster than when the same subject is photographed head-on.

The longer the focal length of the lens, the narrower is the angle of view. The subject seen through a telephoto lens will be moving across the frame more quickly than if the same subject were seen from the same position with a normal lens. For the telephoto lens, therefore, a faster shutter speed will be needed. Similarly, wide-angle lenses allow slower shutter speeds to be used.

### Expressing speed in your subject

Blurring the subject can be used creatively in order to give an impression of speed – a feeling of movement. This can be done by holding the camera firmly and steadily and using a relatively slow shutter speed as your subject passes. In the example that we described of the car driving past, a shutter speed of 1/30 s or even 1/15 s could work well. See Figure 3.1.

Fig. 3.2 A combination of a slow shutter speed and the panning technique has worked very well in this action shot of a cycle race. (Photo: Keith Hawkins.)

The way to take a panning shot is to stand firmly with the legs slightly apart near the place where your subject is going to pass. Let us suppose it is a car. When the subject is approaching, line it up in your viewfinder and swing with it as it passes, keeping the subject as near as possible in the centre of the viewfinder. When it passes you press the shutter button but do not stop the swing through. In fact, your swing should be reminiscent of the golfer's stroke in which he swings right through after actually hitting the ball.

If you try to stop the swing through in a panning shot immediately after you have pressed the shutter release, you will probably stop at the moment of exposure and both subject and background will be badly blurred. The shutter speed you use depends on the speed of your subject but shutter speeds again of 1/30 s or 1/15 s usually give very good results. A typical panning shot is shown in Figure 3.2.

Another most effective means of expressing motion is the technique known as 'panning'. This technique will produce a relatively sharp picture of the subject in motion and the background will be more or less blurred depending on the shutter speed you use. This technique, when carried out properly, can produce a superb impression of speed.

The panning technique requires the camera to follow the movement of the subject and the shutter is released during the movement.

Very fast shutter speeds can show moving subjects very sharply defined in your photograph. A car travelling at 60 miles an hour photographed with a shutter speed of 1/1000 s can be rendered so sharp that it will actually look as if it is stationary. If you want to photograph a moving subject so that it is really sharp, yet still gives the impression of movement, means other than blurring have to be used. An action that has a high point can be nicely frozen with a very fast shutter speed. An example is a horse jumping over a fence. If the moment of exposure is right then in the photograph we can see the horse suspended in the air above the fence. A wave breaking on the rocks at the seaside can be very effective with the water and foam frozen high in the air. The reason we accept such pictures as showing motion is that we know very well from past experience that a horse does not stay still in the air above a fence, nor does water in the form of drops remain up in the air. So with a little thought it is possible to express motion and still have the subject sharply defined.

## The aperture

The aperture of the lens – often called the 'stop' – controls the amount of light getting through the lens. It also affects the appearance of the picture in two ways. It can influence the definition of the lens and it controls the depth of field.

## Lens definition

In general terms, the greater the detail a lens can produce on a film, the sharper the picture will appear. Strictly speaking, the resolving power of a lens is the number of lines per millimetre which it can satisfactorily separate and show individually on the film. To some extent this is an over-simplification because the apparent sharpness of a subject seen in a print depends not only on the resolving power of the lens but also on the resolving power of the film used and the degree of contrast of which the lens is capable. Many lenses today are capable of a far greater resolution than films can record. The final result that we see in a print is the combination of several factors, only one of which is the actual definition of the lens. For practical purposes, however, we think in terms of the 'performance' of a lens.

The performance of a lens is usually best when it is closed down somewhat from its maximum aperture. A lens whose maximum aperture is f/2 may well give its most satisfactory performance at smaller apertures of around f/5.6, f/8 or f/11. This fact means that lenses of very wide apertures and high definition are not easy to design and can be very expensive indeed. By the same token, cheap lenses rarely perform well at their widest apertures.

At very small apertures, definition can deteriorate due to diffraction effects. Again, the cheaper the lens, the greater such effects are likely to be.

Depth of field

Depth of field is in fact an **optical illusion**. If we take up a camera and focus on an object, such as the branch of a tree, then there is only one plane of perfect sharpness in our image and that is the branch on which we have focused. However, if we take a photograph of that branch and then make a print, there will appear to be an area in front of and behind the branch which gives the impression of being in sharp focus. In other words, the picture appears to show a zone of sharp focus stretching from somewhere in front of the point of focus to somewhere behind it. This zone of apparent sharpness is called the depth of field. All objects in that zone of apparent sharpness, with the exception of the point on which we actually focused, are in what is termed **acceptable** focus. That zone of acceptable focus will be greater the smaller the aperture and less the larger the aperture.

Without going into the detailed theory of depth of field, we can say that depth of field is brought about by the fact that if two dots or two lines are brought closer together, there comes a point when the eye no longer distinguishes them as being two separate dots or two separate lines, but regards them as one. Lens standards and depth of field figures are worked out with this consideration in mind.

For practical purposes we can regard depth of field as being governed by:

1. Distance between the subject and the camera. All other things being equal, the further the subject is from the camera, the greater the depth of field. Conversely, the nearer the subject is to the camera, the less the depth of field.
2. Depth of field is controlled by the aperture used. Again, all other things being equal, the wider the aperture, the less the depth of field, and the smaller the aperture, the greater the depth of field.
3. The focal length of the lens also influences the depth of field. The longer the focal length of a lens, the less the depth of field. Conversely, the shorter the focal lens, the greater the depth of field.

Figure 3.3 illustrates the changes in depth of field when the aperture is varied on a 50-mm lens. Figures 3.4–3.6 illustrate the way in which changing the aperture alters the appearance of the photograph and how that appearance is related to the depth of field.

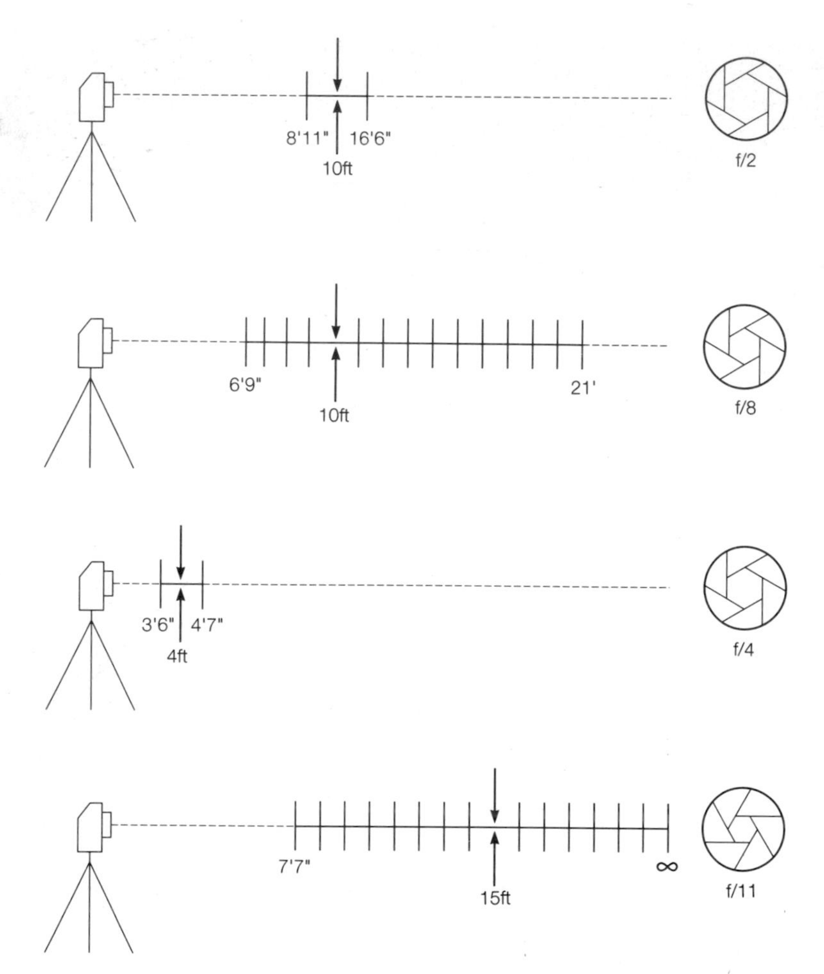


Fig. 3.3 Depth of field at various setting for a 50-mm focal length lens (not to scale).

Hyperfocal distance

The **hyperfocal distance** of a lens at a given aperture is defined as the closest distance from the camera at which objects will be acceptably sharp if the lens is focused at infinity. The infinity setting of the lens is indicated by the symbol ∞. This setting results in a sharp image of distant objects. In practice, an object at infinity may be thought of as the horizon or perhaps something at almost 1000 yards or so from the camera.

As we have seen, the smaller the aperture the greater will be the depth of field. Therefore, the hyperfocal distance at a small aperture will be nearer the camera than when that same lens is set at a wider aperture.

Fig. 3.4 A line up of miniature buses photographed with a very wide aperture. Note that only the middle two buses are in sharp focus.

Fig. 3.5 Use of small aperture has resulted in more buses being sharp; those furthest from the camera being sharper than those nearer.

Fig. 3.6 Use of a very small aperture (f/22) has brought the entire line of buses into sharp focus.

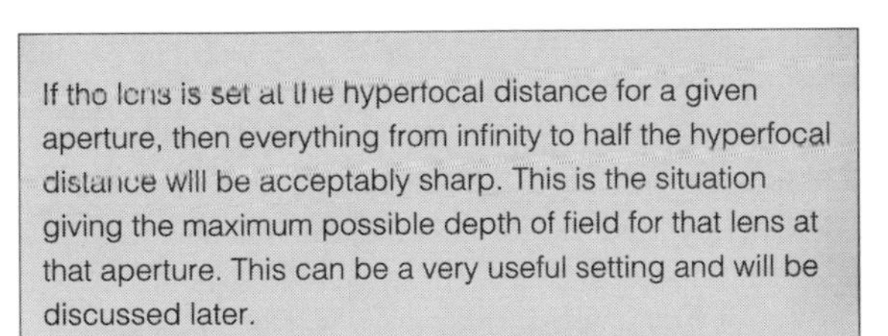

If the lens is set at the hyperfocal distance for a given aperture, then everything from infinity to half the hyperfocal distance will be acceptably sharp. This is the situation giving the maximum possible depth of field for that lens at that aperture. This can be a very useful setting and will be discussed later.

## Making use of depth of field

There are two possible reasons why we may wish to control the depth of field. The first of these is to make sure that as much as possible of our picture is acceptably sharp. The second is to produce a zone of limited sharpness where the subject is sharp and the foreground and background are out of focus.

An example of the first situation would be a beautiful landscape which we are anxious to show in full detail, but would also like to include some object in the foreground, and show it sharply defined. There might, for example, be a gateway at the bottom of a hill which we would like to show sharply defined in the foreground. In this situation we would use the smallest possible aperture in order to achieve the maximum depth of field.

In the opposite situation we might want to take a close-up head and shoulders portrait of a person out of doors but the background is rather distracting. This could be trees or bushes which, if shown sharply behind the subject, would be very distracting. In this situation we would limit the depth of field in two ways: (1) by moving in close to the subject, and (2) by using as wide an aperture as possible. The background would then be thrown out of focus, as shown in Figures 3.7 and 3.8.

Lenses often have a guide to depth of field engraved on their mounts. In Figure 2.23 (page 38) you can see the aperture scale engraved on either side of the focus index mark. This is the depth of field guide.

---

## Exercise

To estimate the depth of field when the lens is set at any given distance, look at the distance figures opposite the two aperture numbers which correspond to the aperture you have set on the lens. For example, if a 50-mm lens is focused on an object at 8 ft, and the aperture is f/11, you can see from the scale that everything will be in acceptable sharpness from about 12½ ft to 6 ft, or if the index mark of the lens is set at 10 ft, then at f/11 everything from approximately 16 ft to 7 ft will be in acceptable focus.

---

If your lens is set at the infinity mark, it is possible to use only one half of the depth of field scale. The mark corresponding to f/16, for instance, is about 8 ft. This would mean that the depth of field at f/16 is approximately 8 ft to infinity when the lens is set on infinity. This hyperfocal distance will be the closest distance that is acceptably sharp when the lens is focused on infinity. Therefore, at f/16 this will be 8 ft. If the index mark on the lens is now moved so that it is on the hyperfocal distance setting, i.e. 8 ft, we will see on the scale that the infinity mark is at f/16 on one side and, on the

Fig. 3.7 A close-up outdoor portrait taken using a small aperture. Depth of field is quite wide and the background, while out of focus, is beginning to show some detail. The subject's shoulders are both sharp.

Fig. 3.8 The same subject taken from the same viewpoint but this time using the widest aperture of the lens (f/1.4). Depth of field is now very limited. Note the virtual elimination of detail in the background. The eye nearest the camera is sharp but the other eye, ear and shoulders are no longer in sharp focus.

other side, the f/16 mark is opposite 4 ft. This means that everything between 4 ft and infinity will be acceptably sharp at f/16.

Some lenses do not have a depth of field scale; this is often the case with zoom lenses because, of course, depth of field changes with focal length. Some zoom lenses have graded markings but if you want to know the actual depth of field setting for your lens at different apertures, or for that matter at different focal lengths, your instruction books should give tables of depth of field settings. Such tables also appear in certain reference books, notably the first and second editions of *The Focal Encyclopedia of Photography*. This is a standard reference work which is available in most good libraries or could certainly be obtained for you through the inter-library loan scheme.

It is possible also to calculate the depth of field using the appropriate formula. Again, a reference work like *The Focal Encyclopedia of Photography* will give you details of these formulae.

You may find that depth of field figures given in tables or those that you calculate for yourself may be a little different from those shown on the markings on your lens. Do not worry about this because depth of field figures vary depending on the standards taken for what is acceptably sharp. Obviously, if we take a very high standard of sharpness, then the depth of field is going to be rather less at any given aperture than it would be for general purpose work.

Do not confuse depth of field with depth of focus. Depth of focus concerns the distance we can move the film plane backwards and forwards while still maintaining a sharp image of our subject. The distance is very small and is measured in fractions of a millimetre. Depth of focus is not important from the practical point of view in using 35-mm cameras, but is relevant in the case of larger format view cameras.

You will find that, in some older textbooks, depth of field is called depth of focus. One easy way to remember the difference is that depth of field refers to anything in front of the lens – i.e. 'out in the field' – while depth of focus is behind the lens.

## Focusing your camera

If you have followed our earlier advice and are now thoroughly familiar with the operation of your camera you will know how to focus sharply on your subject. We shall consider at this point only manual focus cameras. Automatic focusing cameras do present some special problems of their own, and shall be discussed later.

Except with very simple cameras, provision is made to focus the lens on your subject. Some means is provided for the photographer to focus accurately on the subject. In the case of single-lens reflex cameras this can be done on the focusing screen itself and various aids to sharp focus are often incorporated in the viewing screen. Viewfinder/rangefinder cameras often have a rangefinder system incorporated in the viewfinder which is coupled to the lens so that, for example, when two separate images of the subject coincide, the lens is accurately focused. Some cameras do not have a rangefinder system but rely on distance settings of the lens.

Apart from focusing accurately on your subject, advantage can be taken of our knowledge of depth of field to use a technique known as *zone focusing* to make sure a subject is acceptably sharp when we need to focus quickly on that subject and take the picture quickly. You can, for example, set your lens at, say, 15 ft and use an aperture small enough to give a depth of field of a few feet on either side. A wide-angle lens is particularly useful for the zone-focusing technique.

## Pre-focusing

Pre-focusing is very useful in action photography. It is, in effect, a special application of zone focusing. You simply focus your lens at a point on the ground where you know the subject is going to pass. When the subject approaches follow it in the viewfinder and release the shutter when the subject reaches the pre-selected spot.

This technique will work very well using a rangefinder camera. However, if you use a single-lens reflex camera you must press the shutter release just before your subject reaches the pre-selected spot, because with this type of camera there is always a delay between pressing the shutter button and the shutter actually opening. This delay is necessary to allow the mirror to move away and let the shutter blinds open. The delay varies with different cameras but can be around 1/30–1/50 s.

## Automatic focusing

Autofocus cameras are very convenient to use. As we said earlier, they are excellent for most situations. The key to intelligent use of autofocus is to know the characteristics of the autofocus system of the camera you use. Again, much of this information will be in your instruction book. In particular, you should know exactly the area on which the camera focuses. This is usually indicated in the centre of the viewfinder. In the event that you want to focus sharply on a subject which you do not propose to have in the centre of your picture, then one technique is to focus with the subject in the centre of the frame. Then use the 'lock focus' control – usually a half-way-down depression of the shutter release button. Reframe your subject in the viewfinder and then release the shutter. Be particularly aware of things that may upset or deceive the autofocus sensors in your camera.

Taking a picture, for example, through a wire fence at a zoo can sometimes result in disaster because the camera will focus on the wires of the fence rather than on the animal behind. Also be careful when focusing through glass. Again, the autofocus system can, in certain circumstances, focus on the glass rather than the object behind it.

Another problem not always mentioned in instruction books is the possible disturbance of autofocus when using an effects filter on the lens. We shall discuss this later in the chapter on filters, but at this point be particularly careful when using effects filters such as starburst, soft focus or prismatic filters on the lens. These can sometimes completely upset the autofocus mechanism and will lead to out-of-focus pictures. A good general rule when using lens attachments of this kind is to use manual focusing.

### Delays in autofocus mechanisms

The time between setting off the sequence of events for your camera to focus on the subject and taking the picture will vary from model to model. It can be as long as 2 s, and there is a further delay as the mirror of the single-lens reflex must lift out of the way. This additional delay can be anything between 1/50 and half a second. A rapidly moving object could travel a significant distance in that time.

Two possibilities exist therefore. The autofocus lens may not focus quickly enough if the subject is moving and the subject itself may be out of focus before the picture can be taken. Making full use of maximum depth of field is advisable when taking pictures with autofocus cameras. It is, of course, important, too, to know when and how to use the camera in manual-focusing mode.

Recent advances in autofocus technology have brought about substantially reduced delays. One of the fastest autofocus cameras available today is manufactured by Nikon. Autofocus has become very sophisticated and more advanced cameras offer a number of different modes. It is, for example, possible to set your camera so that the shutter fires automatically when the selected subject is in sharpest focus. This can be most useful with photographing wildlife subjects.

Again, it cannot be stressed too strongly that you must be thoroughly familiar with every aspect of the operation of your camera. The more complex the camera, the greater is the need for this knowledge.

## Summary

**In this chapter we have discussed how modern cameras work, and how to use the basic settings of focus, aperture and shutter speed in order to obtain the kind of pictures you want. The advantages and disadvantages of autofocus cameras have also been discussed. Particular stress was placed on being thoroughly familiar with how your camera works and owning and studying your camera's instruction book.**

---

# 4 Film

The fundamental photographic process is to convert those parts of the photographic emulsion exposed to light to finely divided metallic silver which is black. This process is the basis of most commonly used photographic processes.

When you have finished this chapter you will understand how the photographic image is formed, the various kinds of films available and something of their structure.

Broadly speaking, films can be divided into two main categories: those producing black and white or monochrome photographs, and those producing colour photographs. Both kinds of film work in fundamentally the same way.

The light-sensitive emulsion on the film contains salts of the metal **silver**. These salts have the property of being sensitive to light.

In recent years video photography has made its appearance. In this process the image is converted into signals which are stored on magnetic tape or discs. The image is reproduced by playing it back through a suitable device such as a television receiver. The production of motion pictures on video tape is now very common indeed. Still video photography is available but is not yet capable of producing the quality and definition of which the silver image is capable. Actually, still video cameras are being used already by some newspapers because the digital image can easily be sent by the photographer to the newspaper office over the telephone and then, using the latest computer page make-up technology, can be transferred directly to the required position on the page. Generally, however, still video photography is available only for specialist use, but it is likely to become more and more important and accessible to the general user as time passes. One variant is the Kodak CD system in which images taken on conventional film stock are transferred to a compact disc. The images can then be played back and viewed on a television screen or high-quality prints can be made. For the present, however, we shall confine our discussions to the production of silver-based pictures.

Photography – literally meaning 'writing with light' – is made possible by the fact that silver halides will break up when exposed to light and form metallic silver.

These silver halides do not dissolve in water – in other words, they are insoluble. The combination of these two properties –

Silver halides are compounds known as salts which silver can form with the halogen elements. The halogens of importance in photography are chlorine, bromide and iodine. The halides of silver, therefore, are silver chloride, silver bromide and silver iodide. All are sensitive to light, but their sensitivities differ widely.

sensitivity to light and insolubility – make photography possible.

A film can only work if it is sensitive to light. To record the image permanently it must also be capable of treatment to remove its residual sensitivity to light. This sensitivity to light is brought about by the use of silver halides. The insoluble crystals of these substances are suspended in the gelatine of the photographic emulsion. The crystals must be insoluble, because if they easily dissolved in water they would disperse as soon as the emulsion became wet and the structure of the image would vanish. Everyone is familiar with gelatine in the popular dessert, jelly, which is made from gelatine plus various flavourings. Jelly, of course, contains much more water than photographic gelatine, which is very much harder. The gelatine containing the minute crystals of silver halide is coated on a support. This is a transparent base for the film and is made of plastic material. In the past this base was first of all glass plates and, later, celluloid.

In addition to this basic structure the film has a further layer called the anti-halation backing. The purpose of this is to prevent unwanted light-scatter at the back of the film. In Figure 4.1 we illustrate a basic diagram of a black and white film.

The film emulsion consists essentially of crystals of silver halide suspended in the gelatine layer. When the film is processed, during development those crystals of silver halide that have been affected by light are converted to black metallic silver. The halide that is not affected by light and is not converted to silver is later removed during the process known as fixation. Since the black metallic grains of silver will be produced only in those areas affected by light, the appearance of the image on the film will, in fact, be reversed. The light areas of the original subject will appear dark on the film and the areas which were dark and reflected little or no light will appear

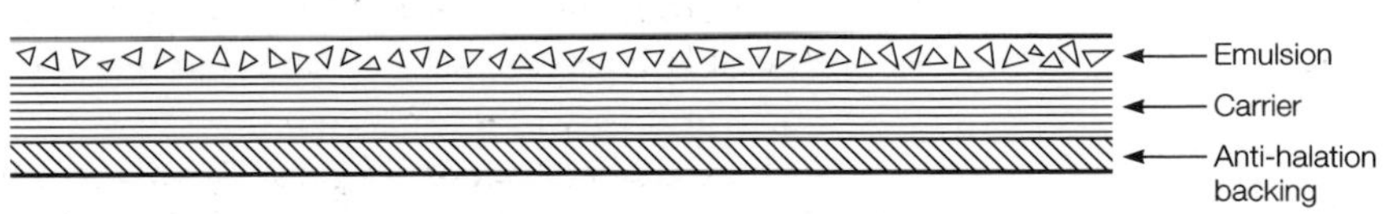


**Fig. 4.1** Cross-section of a black and white film.

clear on the film. Those are the areas in which the unaffected silver halide has been removed. This reversed picture is known as a **negative** image.

In order to produce an image of the original scene, looking as it did when the photographs were taken, it is only necessary to re-photograph the negative. When you do this, the dark areas of the negative become light in the print and the light areas dark, so the tones return to what they were in nature. Figures 4.2 and 4.3 show, respectively, a typical negative and positive made from a photograph. Compare the light and dark areas of each and observe the intermediate tones.

Fig. 4.2 The negative.

Fig. 4.3 The positive.

## Review

**The film base is the carrier and support for the emulsion. It is now made of transparent flexible plastic material but in the past it was made of glass and later celluloid.**

**Celluloid, being flexible, made possible the introduction of roll film cameras which could take a series of pictures on one roll. This, and the discovery that using gelatine as an emulsion carrier**

**had the useful side effect of making much shorter exposures possible, led directly to the invention of cinematography.**

**The anti-halation layer prevents light from being reflected back and degrading the quality of the image. Other layers are also applied to the film during the manufacturing process. A function of one such extra layer is to protect the surface of the emulsion.**

## Film characteristics

Black and white films have four main characteristics which influence the kind of picture they will produce. These characteristics are:

- film speed
- spectral sensitivity
- contrast
- latitude

### Film speed

Film speed refers to the film's sensitivity to light. A film which is very sensitive to light is known as a fast film. Slow films have considerably less sensitivity to light. Not surprisingly, films of a moderate sensitivity to light – which in some ways are the most useful general-purpose films – are termed medium-speed films.

The greater the sensitivity of a film to light, the less exposure it needs. Exposure will be discussed more fully in the next chapter. Film speed is described by a system of speed ratings.

Speed ratings are determined by the film manufacturers and are printed on film packaging and in the instruction leaflets enclosed inside. They are, of course, also given in the manufacturers' technical information leaflets describing a particular film. The main international film speed rating is described as the ISO system (International Standards Organisation). This system has superseded the old ASA (American Standards Association) system and the DIN system (which originated in Germany).

The ASA system is arithmetic – that is, double the film speed is

In general terms, slow speed films vary between ISO 16/13 and ISO 64/19. Medium speed films lie in the range ISO 100/21 to ISO 200/24. Fast films are in the range of 320/26 and higher.

indicated by a doubling of the ASA number. The DIN system is logarithmic and double the film speed is shown by increasing the DIN number by 3. The ISO system combines both arithmetic and logarithmic numbers together to give one composite designation. Table 4.1 presents a series of typical ISO film speeds, together with the equivalent ASA and DIN figures.

You will find that some films are still available in which the speeds are described in the older systems. In all three systems the higher the figure, the faster the film. A film that is rated at ISO 100/21 is twice as fast as a film rated at ISO 50/18 and would require only half the exposure.

**Table 4.1**
Typical film speeds

| ISO | ASA | DIN | ISO | ASA | DIN |
|---|---|---|---|---|---|
| 12/12 | 12 | 12 | 250/25 | 250 | 25 |
| 16/13 | 16 | 13 | 320/26 | 320 | 26 |
| 20/14 | 20 | 14 | 400/27 | 400 | 27 |
| 25/15 | 25 | 15 | 500/28 | 500 | 28 |
| 32/16 | 32 | 16 | 640/29 | 640 | 29 |
| 40/17 | 40 | 17 | 800/30 | 800 | 30 |
| 50/18 | 50 | 18 | 1000/31 | 1000 | 31 |
| 64/19 | 64 | 19 | 1250/32 | 1250 | 32 |
| 80/20 | 80 | 20 | 1600/33 | 1600 | 33 |
| 100/21 | 100 | 21 | 2000/34 | 2000 | 34 |
| 125/22 | 125 | 22 | 2500/35 | 2500 | 35 |
| 160/23 | 160 | 23 | 3200/36 | 3200 | 36 |
| 200/24 | 200 | 24 | | | |

## Spectral sensitivity

The sensitivity of a film to light varies depending on the colour or wavelengths of that light, and/or the characteristics of the emulsion. For instance, a film known as orthochromatic has a very low sensitivity to red light.

In earlier times all films were orthochromatic and red objects appeared very pale indeed on the negative and so reproduced in the positive as black. For example, a person's lips taken on orthochromatic film could appear very dark.

Today general-purpose black and white films are all panchromatic – this means they are sensitive to all colours of the visible spectrum and their spectral sensitivity to those colours corresponds quite closely to that of the human eye. Although colours are reproduced in a black and white print as shades of grey, the tones shown in the print correspond reasonably closely to the brightness that we would expect when looking at those objects in their natural colours. This is why we accept a black and white print as a satisfactory rendition of the real thing. The picture, therefore, appears to us to have the correct range of tones.

Films with special ranges of colour sensitivity are available for special purposes. Orthochromatic films are useful for copying. There are also films that are sensitive to infrared radiation, and these are useful for scientific and other special purposes.

Infrared film, which is available in 35-mm cassettes, can be used to obtain most unusual and indeed surrealistic effects. If we take a picture of a landscape using infrared film but at the same time using a deep red filter over the lens, an unreal effect is obtained because the film responds to infrared instead of light. In prints made from infrared film negatives, deciduous foliage appears white.

Haze scatters light; therefore, pictures taken on a hazy day with ordinary panchromatic film are veiled and indistinct. However, infrared is not scattered by haze so landscapes photographed with infrared film are often spectacularly clear.

### Grain

During development of a film the particles of finely divided metallic silver, derived from the silver halide crystals affected by light, have a tendency to clump together. These metallic clumps of silver give a film its characteristic grainy appearance.

Basically, the larger the crystal of silver halide, the more sensitive it is to light. This means that the slower a film is, the finer the grain will be. Conversely, the faster a film is, the coarser the grain will be. This is a fundamental characteristic of silver emulsions. While some minor modification of graininess can be made, the general rule is that the faster the film, the grainier the image. This is one of the fundamental rules of photography, but one that has been a challenge to photographers over the years and many so-called 'ultra-fine grain' developers have been described which are claimed to produce fine grain results with very fast films. The basic immutable fact, however, is that the degree of graininess of a film is controlled by the manufacturer and the photographer cannot really do a great deal to modify it. In Chapter 9, when we discuss film processing, some techniques will be described which can influence grain. The basic fact remains, however, that the faster the film, the grainier it will be.

Examples of fast films are Ilford HP5 and Agfapan 400. These films, rated by the manufacturer at ISO 400/27, have a coarse-grain structure.

Medium-speed films, such as Ilford FP4 with a speed rating of ISO 125/22 and Agfapan APX 100 with an ISO rating of 100/21, have a medium-grain structure and are ideally suited for most general photography. The fine-grain films, such as Ilford Pan F rated at ISO 50/18, or Agfapan 25 rated at ISO 25/15, have a very fine grain structure indeed and in the 35-mm format are suitable for very big enlargements with the grain being hardly noticeable. For example, a virtually grain free 20 × 16 in. enlargement can be made from such films, whereas grain begins to become clearly discernible in enlargements as small as 8 × 6 in. with ISO 400/27 films. Recently, several manufacturers have produced almost a plethora of new emulsions with claims that new crystal structures and new formulations have enabled them to make substantially finer grain films and faster films with finer grain structures. Undoubtedly improvements have been made but perhaps not quite as great as have been claimed. The photographer must be the judge and the old rule of 'the faster the film, the grainer it is' still applies.

## Contrast

The term **contrast** concerns the relationship between the various tones in a photograph. An average scene is composed of a large number of tones ranging from pure black to pure white. The larger the variety of tones that a film can record, the lower its contrast is considered to be. A film which is of highest contrast, however, can record only a limited number of these tones. Special-purpose films such as those used in the graphic arts industry can be very contrasty, will eliminate all the intermediate tones, and will show everything either as totally black or pure white.

While contrast is one of the inherent qualities of a film it can, nevertheless, be influenced during the development process. We shall see how this is done in Chapter 9.

> In general terms, the slower the film, the more contrasty it is. Medium-speed films have a moderate contrast and fast films have low contrast characteristics. The differences in tones is exaggerated by contrasty film. Thus, a dark grey will become darker and the lighter grey tones will become whiter, thus really increasing the contrast of the original scene. Low-contrast film will bring the greys closer together.

### Latitude

Latitude means how far we can depart from correct exposure and still get a satisfactory print. The more we can over- or under-expose a film and still get a reasonably good picture, the greater the latitude of that film is said to be.

Latitude is another of those film characteristics which is built in during manufacture. In general terms, the faster the film the greater the latitude. Slow films of high contrast have less latitude than fast, low-contrast films. Thus, Ilford Pan F, a slow high-contrast film has less latitude for over- and under-exposure than Ilford HP5 with an ISO rating of 400/27 and low contrast.

All films have greater latitude for over-exposure than they do for under-exposure. Under-exposed negatives are always harder to print than over-exposed negatives.

## How to choose a film

As stated earlier, for most general-purpose work, medium-speed films are best. The slower speed films come into their own when very big enlargements are needed and graininess must be kept to a minimum, but they do need a lot of light. For action shots, when light levels are low, fast films are necessary.

### Colour films

In Chapter 12 we shall discuss colour films in some detail, but here it is sufficient to note that, as in black and white photography, colour films generally available today first produce a black and white negative silver image. By various chemical means colours are produced. How this is done shall be discussed later.

### Chromogenic films

These are films which produce a black and white image but work on the same principal as colour negative films.

The first stage in the production of a negative with this film is the production of the usual negative silver image. By chemical means this silver image is changed to a dye in exactly the same way as the colours in a colour film are produced. The difference here is that the dye is intended to produce a black and white positive print.

The only generally available chromogenic film is Ilford XP2 which can be obtained in both 35-mm cassettes and as 120 roll film. XP2 film is rated at ISO 400/27 but is unique in that it can be exposed over a wide range between ISO 125/22 and ISO 1600/33 and still give satisfactory results. XP2's latitude, therefore, is very wide and it has the unusual ability of recording detail in shadows where other films might lose detail. XP2 has an unusually fine grain structure for a film rated at ISO 400/27.

## Film packaging

Film is usually available in a form that is ready for loading directly into the camera. The 35-mm film comes in cassettes and there are roll films with protective paper backing for larger format cameras. The 35-mm film can also be bought in bulk and loaded by the user into cassettes. This can reduce the cost of film very substantially indeed.

### Information on the packaging

A good deal of information appears on the film packaging. In addition to the name of the film and its manufacturer, there is information on format. For instance, 35-mm film is usually referred to as '135'. The package also gives the number of exposures, the film speed and whether the film is negative or reversal. In the case of colour slide film the colour balance is shown. Also included is a date stamp.

Film will deteriorate with age. The date stamp tells you the latest date beyond which the manufacturer cannot guarantee the film's quality. In the case of black and white film deterioration is slow and substantially outdated black and white film is capable of very good results if it has been stored reasonably well. Outdated colour film, however, deteriorates more rapidly and is always risky to use.

### DX coding

In recent years 35-mm cassettes have been printed with the so-called DX coding. This provides electrically conducting contacts on the outside of the film cassette which are used to transmit information about the film speed to suitable contacts inside certain cameras. This enables the camera's electronic circuitry to set the exposure measuring system to the correct film speed.

## Summary

**In this chapter we have discussed the chemical make-up and structure of black and white film and have generally dealt with film's main characteristics.**

# 5 Exposure

When you have finished this chapter you will be able to understand the meaning of correct exposure, determine the correct exposure for most subjects, use your camera's aperture and shutter speed control to obtain the kind of photograph you want and, at the same time, ensure that the negative is correctly exposed.

## The perfect negative

Producing a perfect negative, or as near perfect as possible, is actually a combination of two things. Firstly, it is necessary to get the correct exposure, which we shall discuss below. Secondly, the negative should be developed in such a manner that optimum results can be obtained. This shall be discussed in Chapter 9.

The aim of these two factors – correct exposure and suitable development – is to produce a negative in which all the important detail is recorded as finely divided metallic silver. This means that the brightest significant highlights, which will be in the darkest areas of the negative, should show details when the negative is printed. The darkest shadow areas of significance should also show detail. These are in the lightest areas of the negative and should be of a density just above that of clear film. All the significant ranges of tone in between should be clearly discernible.

## The right exposure

There are two basic controls on the camera which directly influence the amount of light reaching the film, and thus the exposure. These are:

- shutter speed
- aperture

The shutter speed controls the duration of the exposure and the aperture controls the amount of light passing during the time the shutter is open.

Aperture and shutter speeds are used together to obtain the correct exposure. However, both have their own particular influence on the resulting image. The aperture, as we have seen, controls depth of field, and the shutter speed we use depends on the degree of movement in the subject. It is of vital importance, therefore, to know precisely the kind of result that is wanted and to know how to set the aperture and shutter speed in order to obtain that result.

## Review

**Always remember that aperture and shutter speed work together to produce the final exposure. To keep any exposure constant, if you change one then the other must also be changed to compensate.**

The aperture can be likened to a tap which, when wide open, lets through a large amount of water and, when closed, lets through a small amount of water. The aperture controls the amount of light passing in much the same way.

Both aperture and shutter speed settings have been arranged so that they are in a doubling series. If you look at the shutter speed controls on your camera you will see a series of numbers: 1000, 500, 250, 125, 60, 30, 15, 8, 4, 2, 1. These numbers refer to fractions of a second. The 1000 figure means 1/1000 s; the 125 means 1/125 s. If you look carefully at this series of numbers, you will see that if you take any one number – let us say 1/250 s – then the immediately adjacent numbers are, respectively, one half and double this time. 1/500 s is half the time of 1/250 s and 1/125 s is double the time of 1/250 s.

The reason for this doubling series is that, at least for black and white photography, it is necessary either to double or halve a given exposure in order to make a really significant difference to the negative. In colour photography or specialist black and white photography smaller changes are sometimes necessary and these can be achieved by using intermediate settings. Some camera shutter mechanisms are not capable of being set between marked shutter speeds, but apertures certainly can be.

The aperture numbering system is also a doubling feature. Apertures are referred to as either 'f/' or just 'f' followed by a number. A typical series of numbers which you may see engraved on your lens are f/2, f/2.8, f/4, f/5.6, f/8, f/11, f/16, f/22. The general rule is that the smaller the number, the larger the aperture and, conversely, the larger the number, the smaller the aperture. (Refer to Chapter 2, page 37.)

A rule of the aperture system is that any lens of whatever focal length set to a given aperture will let through the same amount of light as any other lens set to the same aperture.

The exposure-determining systems, therefore, of our camera and lens are doubling systems for both the shutter speed and the aperture. If we know that a correct exposure might be 1/125 s at f/5.6, then we know the correct shutter speed for any aperture or, conversely, the correct aperture for any shutter speed.

### Review

**The correct exposure as measured is 1/125 s at f/5.6. If we open the shutter for twice as long and use 1/60 s it would be necessary to halve the amount of light going through the lens for an equivalent exposure, and this would amount to setting the lens at f/8. For half the shutter speed, that is, 1/250 s, more light would be needed to pass through the lens and we would have to open up to f/4.** **See also Chapter 2, page 37.**

In previous years, before iris diaphragms were in general use, apertures were made by drilling suitably sized holes on a slide. These holes were known as 'stops'. The term 'stop' is often used to describe aperture settings today and the expression 'open up one stop or two stops' means opening up the aperture one or two aperture settings. Exposure is controlled not only by the aperture system but also by the shutter speed, so when we see a reference to increasing exposure by one stop (that is, doubling it), this can be achieved either by opening the aperture one stop or by halving the shutter speed.

The relationship between aperture and shutter speed gives the same exposure, as we have shown in the series above, which means that any of the combinations of shutter speeds and apertures giving equal exposures will produce negatives of the same density. This relationship is known as the **reciprocity law** and holds good over a very wide range of shutter speeds and apertures. Complications can, however, occur when shutter speeds become either excessively short or excessively long. The negatives produced in such cases will be thinner than expected. This phenomenon is known as **reciprocity failure**. In such cases it becomes necessary to give extra exposure to compensate. Film manufacturers publish details of the extra exposure needed under such conditions. For normal work most photographers will have no need to worry about reciprocity failure.

## Film speed and exposure

The faster a film is rated, the less exposure it requires. A film with a speed rating double that of another film will only require half the exposure of the original film. A film of ISO 200/24 is twice as fast as a film of ISO 100/21. If, for example, the correct exposure for a scene using ISO 200/24 film was 1/250 s at f/8, then if we used the ISO 100/21 film for the same scene with no change to the lighting then the correct exposure would be 1/125 s at f/8. Alternatively we could keep the shutter speed at 1/250 of a second and open up the aperture to f/5.6.

### Incorrect exposures

An under-exposed negative looks thin and lacks density. There is very little detail, if any, in the shadow areas. An over-exposed negative is very dense and detail in the highlight areas runs together or becomes 'blocked'. Reasonably satisfactory prints can be obtained from under-exposed and over-exposed negatives provided the degree of over- and under-exposure is not excessive. Just what this degree of over- and under-exposure is depends on the photographic emulsion you are using and how the negatives have been developed. In general terms, a medium-speed black and white film can yield reasonably good prints with a level of under-exposure of 1 to 2 stops and a level of over-exposure of up to 4 stops. This means an exposure range of 2 to 4 times in the under-exposed direction and up to 120 times in the over-exposed direction.

A correctly exposed negative has excellent detail in both shadow and highlight areas and is of good contrast. Figure 5.1 shows a correctly exposed negative. An under-exposed negative, as seen in Figure 5.2, is very thin and lacking in detail in the shadow areas. Figure 5.3 shows an over-exposed negative; here the negative is dense and the highlight areas can become blocked.

When using colour film, exposure latitude is very much less. With colour negative film, just as in black and white photography, there is greater latitude for over-exposure than under-exposure. The reverse, however, is true when making slides. The reversal colour process is much more sensitive to over-exposure and a slightly

> It is always easier to print an over-exposed negative than an under-exposed negative. The latitude for both over- and under-exposure is greater the faster the film. Films such as Ilford HP5 with an ISO rating of 400/27 has considerably greater latitude than Ilford Pan F with an ISO rating of 50/18. Just how much this latitude is for individual films depends, as we shall see, on the way they are developed.

Fig. 5.1 A correctly exposed negative.

Fig. 5.2 An under-exposed negative.

Fig. 5.3 An over-exposed negative.

under-exposed slide will always look better than a slightly over-exposed slide. This shall be discussed further in Chapter 11 on colour photography.

While a certain amount of latitude exists in exposure for colour and black and white films, there is no real substitute for correct exposure. Best-quality pictures result from as near as possible the correct exposure.

## Measuring exposure

Most of the modern cameras have in-camera means of determining exposure, and many do this automatically. Some provide automatic exposure with the capability of overriding the in-camera meter's suggestions and setting the exposure yourself. Others allow you to set the appropriate shutter speed automatically or you can set the shutter speed and the aperture will be set automatically. Such systems are referred to by the following terms:

1. **Shutter priority**. In this method you choose the shutter speed you want to use and the camera's metering system sets the aperture.
2. **Aperture priority**. In this system you select the aperture and the camera will choose the appropriate shutter speed.
3. **Programmed systems**. In these systems both aperture and shutter speed are set automatically by the camera. In the simpler systems the camera usually selects the fastest shutter speed and only reduces this when the maximum aperture has been reached under conditions of diminishing light intensities. More sophisticated automatic systems, however, enable you to 'request' the kind of picture you would like. Thus, for instance, it is possible to set the exposure system to give priority to the small apertures when maximum depth of field is needed – for instance, in landscape photography. Alternatively, for wide aperture work – such as limited depth of field preferences in outdoor portraiture – the camera can be set to give priority to

wide apertures. Another possible option is for the use of fast shutter speeds in action photography. For this kind of work the camera will operate with the fastest possible shutter speeds, the aperture being automatically adjusted to suit.

At least one make of camera offers the photographer a series of small programme cards that can be inserted in the camera back to determine the kind of shutter or aperture priority the photographer requires.

The actual area which the camera chooses to meter varies considerably. In some cameras an overall average meter reading is made; in others larger or smaller areas of the scene are chosen; and still others weight the centre areas and attach less importance to the periphery of the scene. Some cameras give you a choice in the kind of reading preferred. This choice can be very wide and can be quite confusing to the uninitiated.

In whatever ways your camera meter functions, it is absolutely essential that you fully understand its operation. Once again, you are strongly advised to be completely conversant with every aspect of your camera operation and to consult your instruction book whenever necessary.

## Separate light meters

If your camera is not fitted with an exposure-metering system, you will need to use a separate light meter. These meters work in the same way as meters in the camera itself. Such meters will give you suggested aperture/shutter speed combinations from their calculator dials and you simply transfer them to the camera. More sophisticated – and expensive – models will give you a direct digital read-out on a small screen.

Most built-in camera exposure meters measure the light reflected from the subject. Separate meters, however, often have the additional, very useful, facility of measuring the light falling on the subject. This is known as the incident light method of estimating exposure and can be most useful. In the incident light method, the meter is pointed from the subject towards the camera. A white dome or translucent cover is placed over the meter when this is carried out so that the actual light intensity falling on the subject can be measured.

### Your meter is a blockhead

Your meter is not particularly intelligent. It is designed to measure light intensities and to interpret these for you in terms of exposure, in other words, shutter speed/aperture combinations. The meter assumes that you are taking pictures of average subjects. These can be landscapes on a sunny day, buildings in the street, portraits of people, pictures in your garden and in fact a very large range of subjects. All these subjects have one important thing in common: they are composed of areas of light and dark, and if you integrated those areas of light and dark you would have a mid-grey tone.

This overall mid-grey, expressed as 18 per cent grey, is the overall light value that the meter expects to see when it is pointed at the subject. It calculates the exposure necessary to render that subject in the resulting photograph as an 18 per cent grey tone. It is important to understand that this is the way your meter 'thinks' so that you can be sure of getting the correct exposure every time when you are taking pictures of subjects which differ somewhat from the average.

If you were to take a meter reading from, say, a piece of white cardboard, the meter would assume that it was looking at 18 per cent grey and would recommend the exposure that would be necessary to show that piece of white paper as 18 per cent grey. This means that the recommended exposure would be rather less than the correct exposure necessary to show the white paper as being truly white in the print. The difference is about 2½ stops. This means that if you took a meter reading from a piece of white paper and the recommendation was, say, 1/125 s at f/8, you would need to open up the aperture to between f/2.8 and f/4 to get the correct exposure.

The opposite situation obtains when you are measuring the exposure from a darker than normal subject. Suppose you were taking your meter reading from a black-painted wall. Again, the meter would assume that it was looking at something 18 per cent grey and would tell you the exposure needed to show that black wall as mid-grey. In this case, therefore, you would need to give less exposure and so you would move down one or two stops.

## Against-the-light subjects

Taking photographs against the light produces the so-called 'contre-jour' effects. When the meter is pointed towards a light source such as the sun, the meter will be fooled and recommend a shorter exposure than necessary to show proper detail in your subject. Foreground objects, therefore, will appear almost as silhouettes. You can avoid this effect by giving an extra exposure of one or two stops; and some cameras have an 'against-the-light' correction that will do this for you when you press the appropriate button.

Typical situations which are not always straightforward can be handled in a variety of ways. One method is to take a meter reading of the darkest shadow and a meter reading of the brightest highlights and use an exposure half-way between the two.

In practice, a useful guideline is to remember that any scene with large light areas can benefit by giving extra exposure of, perhaps, one stop over the recommended meter reading. Conversely, subjects with large dark areas can be improved by giving less exposure than indicated.

A useful method is to bracket exposures. Take a general meter reading of the subject and expose at the recommended meter reading. Then add one stop more and one stop less than recommended. In extreme cases this can be extended to two stops more and two stops less. If you keep a careful record of your exposures, you can see from the resulting prints which is the most suitable exposure for that kind of subject and note it for future reference.

Another method is to take an incident light reading and use this as the correct exposure. While this method will take into account some of the problems of different reflectivity of subjects you will need to make some correction for more difficult subjects.

You can take a substitute reading from an 18 per cent grey card, making sure that the light falling on the card is the same as the light falling on the subject. You can even use your hand as a substitute. Professional photographers often use this method. Medium-toned Caucasian skin has a reflectance roughly equal to 18 per cent grey. Darker skin, of course, will need compensation and it may be necessary to give less exposure if a substitute reading is taken using a darker skin tone.

## Exposure meter: angle of view

Separate exposure meters often have a fairly wide angle of view, known as the **angle of acceptance**. Some meters in cameras also see rather a wider angle of view than seen by the film. On the other hand, many cameras have meters with restricted angles of view and in some cases these can be very restrictive indeed, enabling metering to be done on small areas of the subject. Extreme cases are the so-called spot meters which allow you to measure luminescences of very small areas of the subject.

If your meter sees a wide angle, bright skies can give rise to under-exposure, and it can be advisable to tip such meters down slightly so that sky areas will not unduly influence the recommended exposure.

### Exposure when taking close-ups

As we saw in Chapter 3, you can take close-up pictures of small objects either by using a macro lens, a supplementary lens or by extending your lens beyond its closest focusing distance by means of extension tubes or bellows. When the scale of reproduction is less than 0.1 (that is, less than 1/10) no correction is needed. For higher values, however, some exposure compensation is necessary to take into account light loss as the lens is extended from the camera body. (Supplementary lenses and some macro lenses do not require exposure compensation because they do not reduce the amount of light falling on the film.) Automatic through-the-lens exposure estimating systems will take care of any necessary correction of this for you. If measuring exposures with the separate meter, however, the necessary correction is given by the formula:

$$\text{True f/number} = \text{Nominal f/number} \times (M + 1)$$

where $M$ is the magnification or scale of reproduction. $M$ is defined as the linear size of the image divided by the linear size of the subject. Full details of the use of this formula can be found in any edition of *The Focal Encyclopedia of Photography*, published by Focal Press.

As with all aspects of camera operation, be sure that you understand fully how your metering system works and how you can override it if necessary. Only in this way can you be assured of correct exposure every time.

---

## Exercise

Load your camera with a medium-speed film. Choose a well-lit average scene such as a landscape on a sunny day. Make your first exposure exactly as indicated by your meter. Call this exposure No. 1; then make a series of exposures, each one half the preceding one. When you have come to the limit of your aperture/shutter speed combinations, go back to the correct exposure, take another picture and make a series of exposures, this time doubling each successive exposure. Develop your film and examine the negatives carefully, noting how details change in the light and dark areas with changes in exposure.

---

## Summary

**In this chapter we have discussed the concept of 'correct exposure' and considered how your meter estimates this. Exceptions to the norm have been described and details have been given on how to cope with these eventualities.**

---

# 6 Filters

In general terms a filter is made of transparent material which is usually placed on the front of a lens. It changes the light passing through the lens in such a way as to change the image recorded on the film.

When you have studied this chapter you will understand how filters work and be able to use filters to modify tones in black and white photographs. Thus you will be able to change the appearance of your photographs by the use of appropriate filters. You will also understand when filters should be used in colour photography. Filters can be divided into three main types:

- tone modification filters
- special effects filters
- colour film filters

## Tone modification filters

As we have already discussed, in black and white photography, colours appear in prints as tones of grey. Today's panchromatic emulsions have a colour sensitivity closely matching that of the human eye. Therefore, colours appear in a black and white print in very similar degrees of brightness that appear to our eyes when we view the original scene. For most subjects the tones appearing in black and white prints are satisfactory and no filter is needed.

Sometimes, however, changing the tone of one colour can help to make the part of the picture containing that colour stand out in greater contrast from the rest of the picture. For example, clouds can appear in similar tones of grey to the surrounding blue sky, and suitable filters can be used to darken the blue of the sky and make the clouds stand out. The colours red and green tend to reproduce in black and white as similar tones of grey. One or the other can be darkened or lightened by the use of suitable filters to make them stand out from each other.

### How filters work

Tone modification filters work by lightening their own colours in a black and white print and darkening other colours. White light is composed of a band of wavelengths in what we call the **visible spectrum**. The spectrum is made up of a wide range of colours extending from deep red to violet. For practical purposes, however,

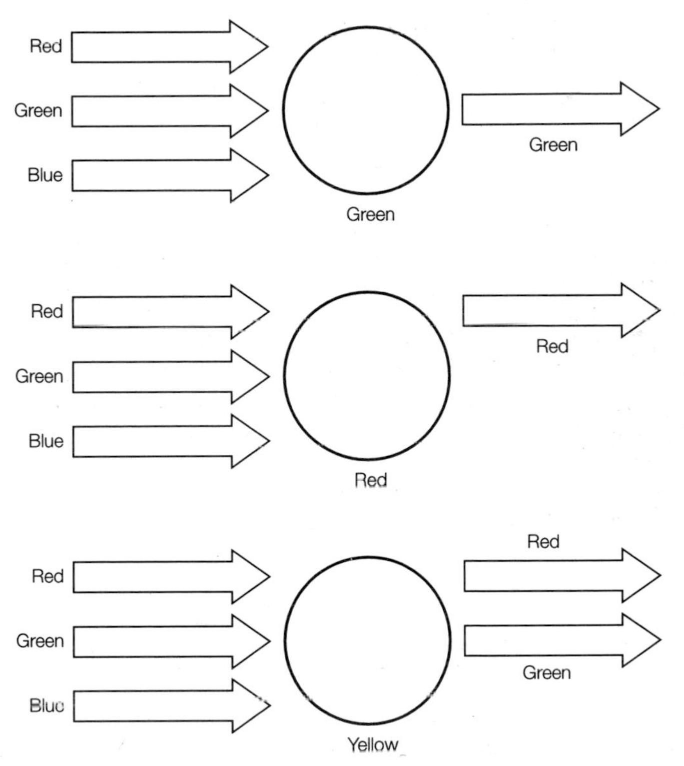


Fig. 6.1 How filters work.

we can assume that white light consists of a mixture of equal quantities of light of the three primary colours: that is, red, green and blue. Things appear to our eyes to be the colour of the light they reflect, or, in the case of transparent objects, of the light they transmit. Other colours are absorbed. Green grass looks green because it absorbs red light and blue light and reflects the green to us. A piece of red glass looks red because it stops the green and blue light and lets only the red light pass through.

If filters worked perfectly, they would allow light of their own colour **only** to pass and hold back completely light of other colours. In practice this is not the case. Filters will let through light of their own colour but tend to reduce rather than eliminate light of other colours. How this works is shown in Figure 6.1.

The effect of using different coloured filters on the appearance of a subject when photographed in black and white is illustrated in the following set of photographs. Figure 6.2 is the key to the colours of the four balls in the photographs and Figures 6.3–6.7 show how those balls look when photographed through various colour filters.

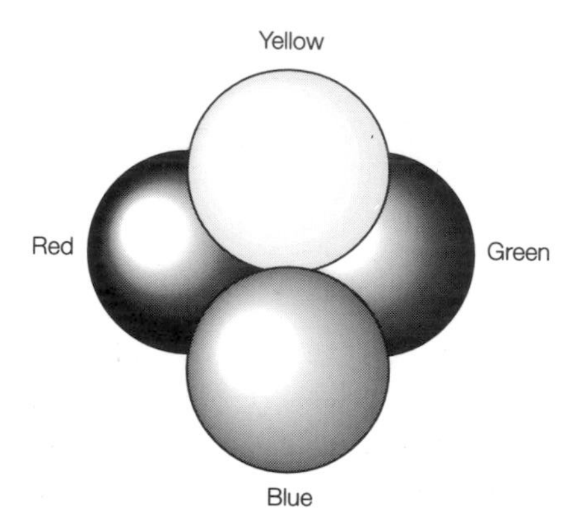


Fig. 6.2 Colour key

Fig. 6.3 The four balls shown in our diagram photographed with no filter on the camera lens.

Fig. 6.4 Using a yellow filter.

Fig. 6.5 Using a red filter.

Fig. 6.6 Using a green filter.

Fig. 6.7 Using a blue filter.

## Practical use of filters

Suppose we wish to make the clouds in a landscape stand out more clearly against the sky. The sky is blue, but we would like to darken it. The answer is to use a green filter or a red filter, both of which will darken the blue. It is also possible to use a yellow filter. Because yellow is made up of a mixture of red and green it will also absorb blue light to some extent. So by using any of these three filters, blue will be held back and so darkened in comparison with the clouds. The deeper the colour of the filter we use, the greater will be the effect and, so far as darkening skies is concerned, red filters are particularly useful.

A word of warning! The sky must be really blue if the filters are to have an affect. It is quite useless, for instance, to try to darken the clouds of an overcast sky with a colour filter.

**Colour must be present if it is to be darkened by an appropriate filter.**

Another example might be to separate red and green tones in a scene. A red tomato among green foliage is one example. The photographer could use two alternatives. Firstly, a red filter could be used which would lighten the tomato and make the green leaves appear darker; or a green filter could be used which would make the tomato look darker and the green leaves lighter.

See also the discussion on the use of the colour triangle in Chapter 11, page 143. The colour triangle provides a very simple and handy method of working out what filters will do to their own and other colours.

### Review

**Remember that filters lighten their own colours and darken the other colours in black and white photography. Thus red lightens red and darkens blue and green. Green darkens reds and blues and lightens its own colour. Blue filters will lighten blue objects but darken reds and greens, and as a mixture of red and green makes yellow, they will, of course, also darken yellows.**

## Filters and exposure

Filters usually reduce the intensity of light passing through them. The deeper the filter, the greater this reduction in intensity. If the amount of light filters absorb is more than about one-third of a stop, then some exposure compensation is necessary. The amount of that compensation is known as the **filter factor**. These factors are expressed as 2×, 3×, 4× and so on. The deeper the filter, the higher its factor. A factor of 2× means that we need to double the exposure or open up one stop. 3× is triple the exposure so we need to open up 1½ stops. 4× means four times the exposure necessitating an increase of two stops. If your camera uses a through lens metering system, then suitable exposure compensation is done automatically. This is because the camera meters the light falling on the scene through the lens and through the filter which is covering the lens. If, however, you are using a separate light meter you will need to make the appropriate compensation when setting the exposure on the camera.

Best results are obtained when exposure is correct. Over-exposure often negates the effect of a filter. So trying to darken that blue sky just may not work if the exposure is excessive.

### Neutral density filters

These filters are extremely useful if you want to reduce the light reaching your film without reducing the aperture or using a faster shutter speed. Neutral density filters simply cut down the intensity of the light without changing its tonal quality or colour balance. They are available in various densities, usually in steps of 1, 2, 4, 8 times, etc.

## Special effects filters

These filters, like neutral density filters, do not alter the tones or colour balance of the subjects. However, they do change the optical characteristics of the image to a greater or lesser extent. An example is starburst filters. These produce star-shaped images from point sources of light. They are composed of fine crossed engraving on the filter surface. Two star points are produced by one set of lines engraved at right angles. Additional points are added to the stars by additional sets of engraved lines. Other examples include prismatic filters which give multiple images of your subject, graded tone filters and, of course, polarising filters which polarise light.

### Polarising filters

These are available as linear and circular types. The linear type of polarising filter is the most useful for general photography and can be used to reduce reflections from non-metallic materials, such as wood, glass, plastics, water, etc. They can be used to darken areas of the blue sky by reducing scattered polarised light. Their effect is greatest at right angles to the sun. The effects of polarising filters can be observed in an SLR by rotating them in their mounts, and most have special provision for this. With non-reflex cameras, the effects can be observed by looking through the filter while turning it, then taking care to place it over the camera's lens at exactly the required angle. Polarising filters have a fairly high filter factor around 4×. Circular types of polarising filters have applications in beam-splitting devices used in autofocus and automatic exposure-measuring systems.

### Soft focus filters

These filters are most useful for portrait work, particularly with older subjects, because they tend to smooth out facial blemishes and wrinkles. These filters are engraved with concentric circles.

## Colour film filters

### Conversion and light-balancing filters

These are filters which are used with colour film to make sure that the colour of the light is matched to the film in use. For example, photographs taken on daylight colour film using tungsten lighting have a yellowish-red cast. This can be corrected by filtering out the yellow with a blue filter. Such correction filters are discussed more fully in Chapter 11 on Colour.

### Filter fittings

Lenses are usually provided with a screw thread in the front which will take circular filters, lenses, hoods and other accessories. Circular filters in the appropriate size to fit popular lens threads are available. The excellent B&W Program Filter Series is one example. Also there are available a number of filter systems which consist of an adaptor to screw onto the lens and a filter holder which goes onto the adaptor. These filter holders take square-shaped filters of various kinds. Hoya and Chromotech are two examples of such systems. One advantage of the filter systems is that the same filter can be used with various sized lenses simply by using the appropriate adaptor.

### UV and Skylight filters

UV or Skylight filters are useful in cutting out excessive blue in snow scenes, mountain shots and beach scenes. They will cut down ultraviolet light which can record blue on colour film but has no discernible effect in black and white. However, a UV filter is useful to keep permanently on your lens. It is an inexpensive accessory and serves to protect your lens from damage. Another most useful accessory is a lens hood which also usually screws into the filter thread on the front of the lens or even into the filter thread on the front of a filter. These serve to prevent stray light reaching your lens and so reduce the risks of flare spoiling your pictures.

## Summary

**The functions of various types of filter have been described. These include colour filters, effects filters and polarising filters. The use of filters in black and white and colour photography has also been discussed.**

# 7 Light

When you have finished this chapter you will be able to understand how different kinds of light affect the appearance of a photograph and you will be able to use artificial light to create the kind of effects you want.

## Major characteristics of light

The main characteristics of light which are of importance to the photographer are:

- intensity of light
- direction of light
- diffusion of light
- colour characteristics of light

The first three of these characteristics have an important influence on all photographs. The fourth characteristic, colour, is usually only of importance when taking colour photographs.

### Intensity of light

The brightness of light, or its intensity, determines the exposure. Out of doors the natural light comes from the sun. The sun sends out light rays in straight lines in all directions. When these light rays are blocked by some solid object shadows are formed. The shadows formed by bright sunlight have sharp edges because the sun is very far away and is in fact virtually a point source. Out in space the shadows are completely black and are not illuminated. On earth, however, the shadows are lit by diffused light of a rather lower intensity.

The sky is an enormous secondary light source. When the rays of the sun pass through our atmosphere some of the light is scattered and so illuminates the shadows. In addition some light is also reflected into the shadows from objects nearby.

The relative intensity of direct sunlight and the light which illuminates the shadows depends very much on local weather conditions and the latitude in which we live. For example, in temperate climates, where there is a good deal of mist in the air, the difference between direct bright sunlight and open shadows will probably be found to be in the region of three to four stops. Under clear conditions near the equator, differences of as much as eight or nine stops may be observed.

When the sun is obscured by cloud, on an overcast day, then the sky itself becomes the only light source but with a greater intensity in the region obscuring the sun. Hardly any shadows will be observed. The actual intensity of the light will depend on the thickness of the cloud.

### Lighting contrast

The difference in the intensity of light between the sunlit and shaded parts of the subject is the contrast of the lighting.

Our eyes are very adaptable and we can often see into shadows when the light is very contrasty. Films are not always able to do this, and compromises are therefore necessary. When the lighting contrast is in the region of sixteen stops, most black and white films can cope perfectly well with that range of light intensity. Colour films, however, often have less latitude and care must be taken to avoid excessive lighting contrast.

## Direction of light

The direction of the light on the subject is important if we wish to give an impression of texture and depth in the picture. For many subjects very satisfactory results can be obtained with the sun behind the photographer, illuminating the subject at approximately 45 degrees. This shows up textures and the shadows give a pleasant three-dimensional effect. Indeed, this kind of lighting mimics the way that we prefer to see things lit in nature.

Side lighting can be very effective in accentuating texture. This sort of lighting, with the sun at 90 degrees to the subject, produces sharp highlights in raised areas and shadows in depressed areas and so places a much greater accent on the texture of the subject; for example, the surface of a rock or the texture of rough cloth.

### Diffusion of light

Diffused light produces very little in the way of shadows. Portraiture on an overcast day can be very effective because problems like heavy shadows under the eyes and under the chin are largely eliminated.

When the sun is behind clouds, contrast is much reduced and so subjects can fall well within the latitude of the film.

Diffused lighting, however, does not show up texture and buildings and landscapes tend to look less interesting in the photograph. In colour photography, colours appear less saturated.

### Colour quality of light

In colour photography the colour quality of the light is important. This is fully discussed in Chapter 11.

## Available light

Available light is a general term used to describe light which is usually of rather low intensity and is largely outside the control of the photographer. It includes subjects such as a person or object photographed indoors when lit only by light entering the room through a window. It includes the interiors of rooms lit by ordinary domestic lighting and also includes performances on stage lit only by the stage lighting.

Available light, therefore, is usually of low intensity and can be very contrasty. Nevertheless, available light pictures can be very rewarding and can be full of atmosphere.

It is generally suggested that when taking available light photographs, exposure should be based on the highlights and the shadows should be left to take care of themselves. Again, in general terms, this means that moody atmospheric pictures are obtained with little or no detail in the shadows and the highlights are clearly recorded on film. If you expose correctly for the main subject, then in most cases a pleasing result will be obtained. The bracketing method is particularly useful in available light photography.

### Pushing your film

When available light situations are such that the light intensity is too low even for a moderately fast film, it may be desirable to increase the ISO rating of your film. This can be done by push-processing, which involves giving the film longer development. Doubling the ISO rating or even increasing it four or eight times is possible. There is always a loss of quality, however, and graininess does increase. This may not be a bad thing as the increase in grain can add to the atmosphere of the scene. Black and white films and colour slide films can be push-processed quite easily but colour negative films are rather more difficult. Details of push-processing appear in Chapter 9.

With the advances in emulsion technology, very fast films are now available and the push-processing techniques are no longer as significant as they once were.

## Artificial light

The use of artificial light in photography gives the photographer complete control over various characteristics of light, including intensity, degree of diffusion, direction and colour temperature.

The photographer has two main kinds of artificial light available:

- tungsten lighting, sometimes known as incandescent or half watt lighting
- flash lighting

### Tungsten lighting

Various types of tungsten lighting are available to the photographer.

- **Ordinary household lighting.** These can be household bulbs, usually of high intensity, of around 100 or 150 watts. Intensity from the photographic point of view is low but they can be used with great effect.
- **Professional studio lamps.** These are high intensity tungsten lights. They are quite expensive but have a long life. Projection lamps of various kinds are also used.

- **Photoflood bulbs.** These look like ordinary household bulbs but are 'over run'. They have a very high light output but a rather short life – usually about two to three hours. They also get very hot.
- **Tungsten–halogen lamps.** These bulbs are of very high intensity and tend to run very hot. Fittings that use these lamps often have a built-in cooling fan. Many available today are designed for video or movie photography but are just as suitable for taking still photographs.

Incandescent lighting is continuous. The hot bright light that is produced is sometimes hard on the subjects and is no longer very popular in studio portrait work. The great advantage of tungsten lighting is that its characteristics can be seen very easily and its illumination of the subject can be readily adjusted. This makes it ideal for still life subjects.

### Flash lighting

Flash provides a short intense burst of light. It overcomes some of the disadvantages of incandescent lighting but because the light pulses last such a short time it is not possible – or is at least very difficult – to see the effect of flash lighting without some form of supplementary lighting coming from the same position. In studio flash lighting equipment such secondary light sources are known as modelling lights.

Two types of flash are available:

- electronic flash
- flash bulbs

We shall discuss the use of flash lighting in Chapter 8.

## Using artificial light

The effects that can be obtained using artificial light are virtually limitless. In general terms, the kind of lighting that is obtained

By the end of this section you will understand how to use some of the main kinds of artificial lighting in order to obtain the result you want.

depends on the type of reflectors, lenses, fittings and so on that are used with the light source – that is, incandescent bulb or flash tube. The general principles that we are going to discuss are exactly the same whether we use incandescent lighting, flash bulb or electronic flash tubes.

The main types of lighting equipment are given below.

## Spotlights

These lights give a very directional beam of light, rather like direct sunlight or the beam of light obtained from a slide projector (Figure 7.1). Many spotlights allow the beam to be focused and to be changed from a very narrow beam of light to a considerably wider one. Basically, a spotlight consists of a projector type bulb, a reflector and a simple lens system. Spotlights produce sharp and deep shadows like sunlight. They are the mainstay of theatrical lighting and were for many years extensively used in studio photography. They were supplanted largely by the convenient electronic flash umbrella lighting. Recently, fitted with electronic flash tubes, they are enjoying something of a comeback.

## Floodlights

These lamps (see Figure 7.2) produce a broader beam than spotlights so the shadows are neither quite so clearly defined nor as deep. No focusing arrangements are provided. They are useful for portrait lighting.

## Diffused floodlights

Diffused floodlights (Figure 7.3) have a much bigger reflector than ordinary floodlights and are often provided with a mask in front of the bulb to prevent direct light from the bulb falling onto the subject. They are used particularly as fill lights or to produce very soft even illumination. Shadows cast by diffused floods are vague and ill-defined.

## Umbrella lighting

Excellent diffusion is obtained by reflecting light from the inside of a special umbrella. The umbrella is either white or made of

Fig. 7.1 A spotlight.

Fig. 7.2 A floodlight.

Fig. 7.3 A diffused floodlight.

Fig. 7.4 Umbrella lighting. (Photo: Paterson-Photax Group Ltd.)

reflecting fabric. It gives a very diffused light but when using the metallised surface, shadows can be quite sharp. Umbrella lighting (Figure 7.4) has become very popular with studio photographers and is used mainly with electronic flash although it can be used with other light sources.

### Reflectors

Reflecting surfaces can be very useful in photography because they can be employed to reflect light into the shadow areas of the subject and so reduce contrast. Virtually any reflecting surface can be used. Mirrors, a piece of white cardboard or a sheet of crinkled aluminium foil all make useful reflectors. Survival blankets, which are available at most sports stores, are made of highly reflective plastic and are particularly good reflectors.

## Setting up artificial lights

Setting up and using artificial lights really becomes quite simple if you bear in mind one or two basic principles. These basic principles give the photographer a starting point, can help to avoid difficulties, and when fully understood will enable you to try out various kinds of lighting and so obtain the sort of picture that suits the subject.

### Main or key light

The key light is the light that sets the whole tone of your picture and determines exactly where the shadows and the highlights will be. The key light should always be set up first. The starting point that should be borne in mind is that we prefer to see objects lit by a

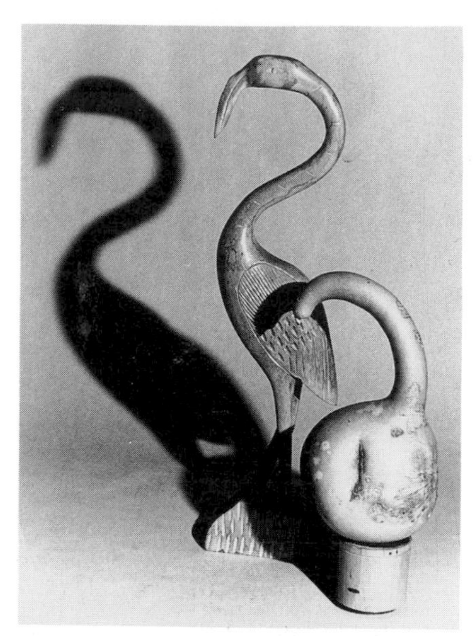

Fig. 7.6 A carved wooden bird and a gourd lit by one light at a 45 degree angle.

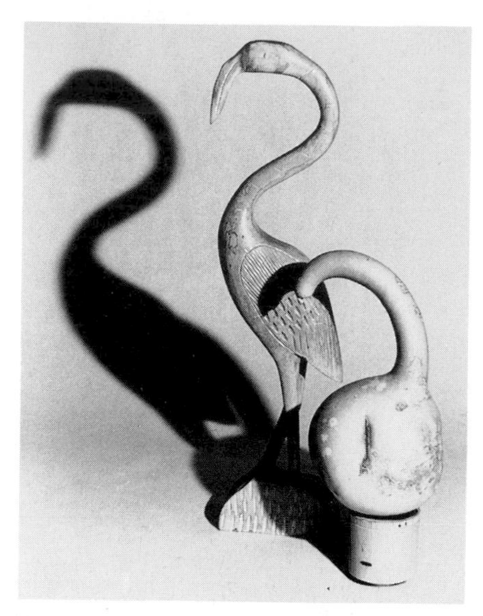

Fig. 7.8 One light at a 45 degree angle plus a reflector board which has opened up the shadows to some extent.

Fig. 7.10 The subject is now lit by one diffused floodlight at approximately the position of the camera.

Fig. 7.11 Subject lit by the original main light at a 45 degree angle as in Figure 7.7 but is also lit by the diffused floodlight as in Figure 7.10. This serves as a fill-in light and provides detail in the shadows by reducing contrast.

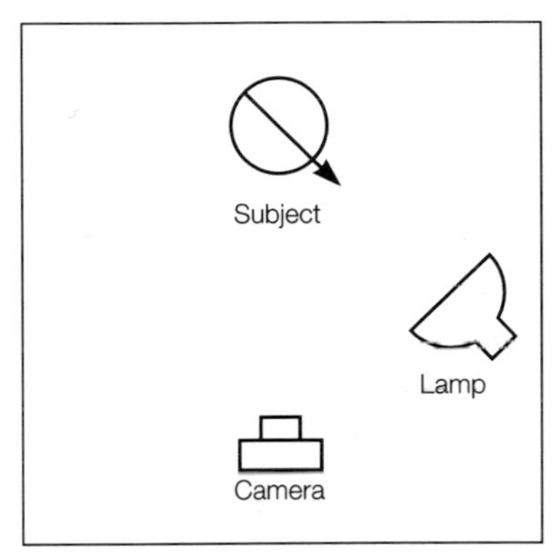


Fig. 7.5 Basic lighting.

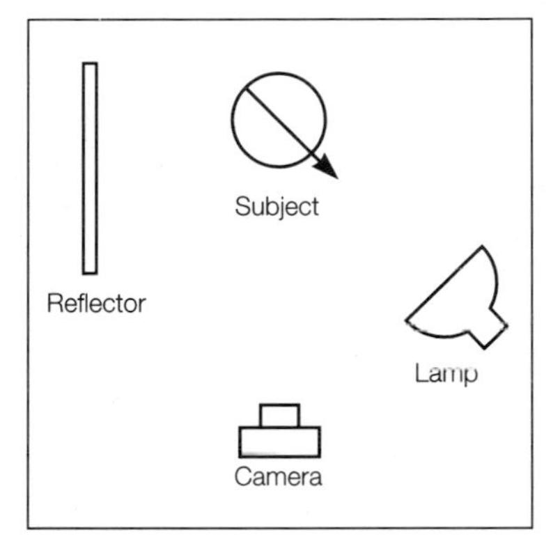


Fig. 7.7 Basic lighting.

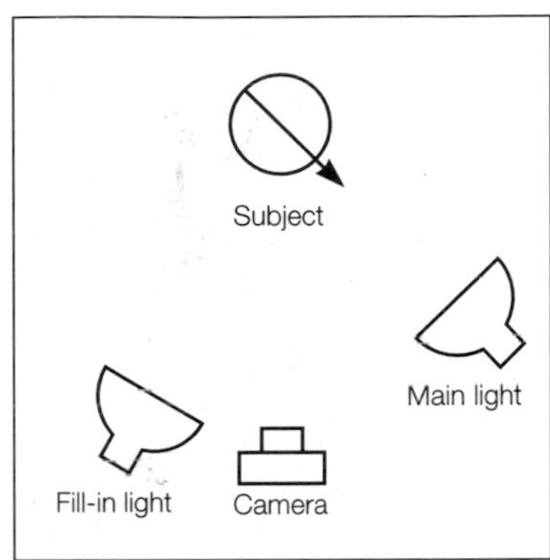


Fig. 7.9 Fill-in light.

single light that is fairly high and casts one set of shadows. More often than not we prefer to look at things with the sun behind us, but perhaps a little off to one side or the other. Thus, try your first artificial light picture with your key light reasonably high, say 2 or 3 ft above the camera height and at about 45 degrees to the line between the subject and the camera. Figure 7.5 shows this type of arrangement. A picture taken with lighting like this is shown in Figure 7.6.

As you can see, the shadows are clearly defined and produce a good three-dimensional effect. This effect is sometimes known as modelling. The picture looks natural and satisfying. If we were to use two lights on opposite sides of the camera, then two sets of shadows would be formed and the effect would be disturbing. The reason it is disturbing is because, as we have mentioned previously, we are used to seeing objects lit by one light: the sun.

One light tends to give dark and heavy shadows. You can make these lighter by using a reflector to reflect back some of the light from your key light onto the shadow side of the subject. Figure 7.7 shows how this is done and Figure 7.8 shows the effect.

## Fill-in light

A more effective means of lightening the shadows is to use a diffused light source such as a diffused flood and to position it so that it will lighten the shadow side of the subject while casting little or no shadows of its own. One of the best ways of doing this is to position the fill-in light as near as possible on the line from the camera to the subject, perhaps a little bit higher than the camera so that any shadow formed by the fill-in light will fall behind the subject and be out of view of the camera, or will be shielded from the camera by the subject. Figure 7.9 shows this arrangement. Figures 7.10 and 7.11 show the kind of light produced by the fill-in light alone and its effect when used with a main light to lighten the background and emphasise the shadows.

## Relative intensities of lights

You can change the intensity of a light by moving it either closer to or further from the subject. Remember that light on your subject will change very rapidly as you alter its distance. The intensity of the light is actually proportional to the square of the distance between the light and the subject, so that if you double the distance between a light and the subject then the intensity of the light will reduce to one-quarter, four times the distance and the intensity is reduced to one-sixteenth. While it is useful to understand the **inverse square law**, as it is called, in practice it is easier to measure the intensity of the light falling on the subject by means of an exposure meter.

In black and white photography, pleasing effects can be obtained with the fill-in light being between one and three stops lower in intensity than the main light. This means, of course, that the fill-in light could be between one-half and one-eighth of the intensity of the main light. Colour film has much less latitude than black and white film and so it cannot handle as much contrast. Therefore, the difference between the main and fill-in light should be no more than a half to one stop.

## Setting up lights

When setting up lights, each one should be set up separately and its intensity measured. In the case of our example, set up the key light first and measure the intensity of the light or the exposure with an exposure meter. Turn off the key light, position the fill-in light and measure its intensity (exposure). Adjust the position of the fill-in light until the difference between it and the main light gives you the desired ratio. Finally, turn on both lights and again measure the exposure. Usually you will find that the exposure is determined by the key light, and the fill-in light will only contribute a small amount of additional illumination to the final light intensity.

## Summary

**Photography literally means 'writing with light'. In this chapter we have discussed how light can be best used to obtain the kind of photographic results we require and look pleasing to the eye.**

---

# 8 Flash Photography

When you have studied this chapter you will have a working knowledge of the different kinds of flash lighting currently available and will be able to produce satisfactory photographs using them.

## Kinds of flash

As we have already mentioned, flash lighting produces a very short but intense burst of light. There are two kinds of flash currently in use: flash bulbs and electronic flash.

### Flash bulbs

Figure 8.1 is a diagram of a typical flash bulb. These bulbs are disposable – they are fired once, then thrown away – and are available singly, like the bulb illustrated, or as several on a flash bar or sometimes as four together in a flash cube. Flash bulbs contain a foil or very fine wire, which is inside a glass bulb in an atmosphere of oxygen. The foil or wire consists of aluminium, magnesium or other inflammable metal which is in contact with a filament covered with an explosive paste. The bulb is fired by passing a low-voltage electric current through the filament. This causes the explosive to fire, which in turn ignites the wire and produces a flash of light. This flash lasts for between 1/200 and 1/20 of a second according to the type of bulb.

There is a delay between the current being applied and the time when the flash reaches its maximum intensity. For small flash bulbs the delay is about 20 milliseconds. For larger ones, usually designated Class S, there is a delay of around 30 milliseconds or more. In addition, there are extra long burning flash bulbs available called Class 'FP' especially for use with focal plane shutters.

Flash bulbs may be fired in special flash guns which have a synchronising wire connected to the camera or, in the case of flash cubes and flash bars, may be fitted directly onto the camera. Many cameras have two flash sockets marked 'M' and 'X'. The 'M' socket has a built-in delay so that the bulb is allowed to reach its maximum output before the shutter opens.

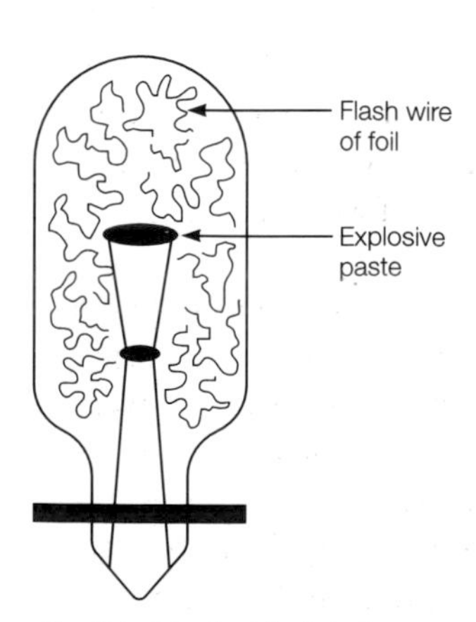


Fig. 8.1 A typical flash bulb.

Flash bulbs are an excellent form of artificial light. They are available in either clear or blue glass which means that they can be used with colour film balanced for daylight. Flash bulbs can produce light of very high intensity indeed, but they are relatively expensive.

## Electronic flash

Electronic flash, known in America as 'strobe', is a stroboscopic development originally developed by the American scientist and photographer Dr Harold Edgerton.

Electronic flash is really an electric spark rather like a flash of lightning. It takes place in a small tube which is filled with a rare gas such as xenon or krypton. Two separate electric circuits are used in an electronic flash gun. One circuit produces a very high voltage of the order of several thousands of volts which is applied across two electrodes in the electronic flash tube. The second circuit, which is of a very much lower voltage, is called the triggering circuit. A wire in this triggering circuit is wound round the flash tube. When an electric pulse is applied to the trigger circuit it causes some ionisation of the rare gas making it more conductive of electricity and so allows a spark to flash between the two electrodes.

Electronic flash tubes can be fired over and over again and so are very much cheaper in use and more convenient than flash bulbs.

A characteristic of electronic flash is virtually no delay in firing. Immediately the circuit is closed the flash fires. The electronic flash lasts for a very short time. Depending on the characteristics of the tube and the circuitry, electronic flash duration can vary between 1/200 and 1/50 000 of a second. Thus electronic flash is useful for freezing fast motion.

As electronic flash has a colour temperature similar to daylight, it can therefore be used with colour film balanced for use in daylight.

Today, an enormous number of different types, sizes and powers of electronic flash guns are available. Some are simple units; and others offer automatic exposure control, which works by measuring the light reflected back to the flash gun from the subject and turns the flash light off when it has been on long enough for correct exposure.

There are also the so-called 'dedicated' flash guns. These are flash guns that are designed to work with a specific camera. Parts of the circuitry that operates the flash gun are included in the camera so that the two work together to produce correctly exposed pictures.

### Synchronisation of electronic flash

Because the production of an electronic flash is virtually instantaneous, and because the flash itself is of extremely short duration, special arrangements have to be made for synchronisation. The 'X' setting on your camera is the one to use for electronic flash.

So-called 'X' synchronisation means that the flash fires when the shutter is fully open and that there is no delay in the circuitry. As we have seen in the case of flash bulbs, the delay is provided to enable the bulb to produce its maximum light output. Thus, when the 'M' synchronisation setting is used, the camera will close the flash contacts a short time before the shutter opens. Use of this kind of synchronisation with electronic flash units means that the flash will have occurred and will have been extinguished before the shutter has even begun to open.

## Types of shutter and flash

Basically there are two kinds of shutters in use. These are the so-called 'between the lens shutters' or 'leaf shutters' and 'focal plane shutters'. Leaf shutters, as their name implies, are usually composed of a number of leaves which open and then close. The shutter speed is the duration for which the leaves remain open. With this kind of shutter, at every speed there is a point where the shutter is completely open. So, in the 'X' synchronisation position, contact is made at this point – when the shutter is fully open. With these shutters electronic flash can be used at any setting. The maximum shutter speed of leaf shutters is usually no more that 1/500 s.

### Focal plane shutters

Focal plane shutters consist of two blinds. In the slower speed ranges the first blind opens fully. At the end of the exposure period the second blind closes. Faster shutter speeds are achieved by letting the second blind start closing before the first blind has fully opened.

What actually happens is that the film is scanned by a slit, i.e. the distance between the two blinds. The narrower this slit, the shorter the exposure. This arrangement means that at the faster shutter speed some of the film area will always be covered.

Since electronic flash is of very short duration, electronic flash can only be used with focal plane shutters up to the maximum speed at which they expose the whole of the film area. Cameras fitted with focal plane shutters usually have a symbol on their shutter speed dials which is the recommended shutter speed setting for use with electronic flash. For most cameras this is of the order of 1/60 s. Some recently developed focal plane shutters, however, offer electronic flash synchronisation at higher shutter speeds of 1/125 s and in other cases 1/250 or even 1/500 s and less have been described.

### Review

**If an electronic flash picture is taken with a camera fitted with a focal plane shutter set at too fast a shutter speed then part of the frame will be exposed correctly and part will be blank.**

## Flash exposures

Flash exposure can be determined manually using guide numbers or automatically with automatic electronic flash units. Exposure can also be determined with flash meters.

### Guide numbers

Guide numbers link film speed to the aperture and distance between flash and the subject. For flash bulbs, guide numbers are also determined by the shutter speed. As we have seen, flash bulbs emit a pulse of light which lasts quite a long time. Obviously, if you use a fast shutter speed, then you will use just a slice of that light output. Guide numbers are published by flash bulb manufacturers and are

Suppose, with a certain film, the guide number is 56 (feet). To use the flash 10 ft from the subject we would need an aperture of:

$$\frac{GN}{d} = \frac{56}{10} = 5.6, \quad \text{i.e. f/5.6}$$

Many flash units have a calculator dial or table which enables you to read off the correct aperture immediately.

usually given on the outside of the flash bulb packages or in literature on the use of flash bulbs.

In the case of electronic flash the guide numbers appear in the table or calculator dial usually on the side or back of the unit. At any given ISO rating for correct exposure the guide number is:

$$\text{Guide number (GN)} = \text{f/number} \times \text{distance (d)}$$

Guide numbers can be expressed in both metres and feet, depending on which unit you use to measure the distance. They are mathematically accurate because flash obeys the inverse square law just like other light sources.

The guide number formula can be used to calculate either the correct distance of the flash from the subject for a given aperture or the f/number required for a given distance.

### Automatic exposure

Automatic electronic flash units have a light sensor and circuit which measures the amount of light reflected by the subject and cuts off the flash when the correct exposure has been reached.

Since the sensor works exactly the same as an exposure meter, it will give the correct exposure for average subjects. Non-average subjects, however, need the same corrections as when using an exposure meter; therefore, if your subject is light, give more exposure, if your subject is dark, give less exposure.

## Using flash light

In general terms, the principles of illumination apply whether you are using incandescent lighting, flash bulbs or electronic flash. Flash has an inherent disadvantage in that most flash guns and flash fittings are designed to be attached to the camera. This gives perfectly satisfactory results for 90 per cent of snapshot subjects but the kind of illumination produced by on-camera flash has important disadvantages. The frontal lighting it produces is very flat. A heavy

The red eye which often spoils flash portraits is due to light reflecting off the retina of the eye back to the camera and, of course, shows up the colour of the retina. This reflection is usually of no great disadvantage in black and white photography but can ruin colour pictures.

**Warning for City & Guilds candidates.** City & Guilds do not like to see obvious use of on-camera flash, terming it 'insensitive use of flash'. Avoid on-camera flash, therefore, unless your picture is so important that it does not matter how it was taken!

Fig. 8.2 Portrait taken using on-camera flash. Note the flat lighting effect and harsh shadows on the left behind the subject.

shadow is often cast behind the subject (Figure 8.2), and it can produce the so-called 'red eye' effect.

Flash photography can be improved in a number of ways. The first of these is to take the flash off the camera. This can be done by using an extension lead of about 2 to 3 ft long and holding the flash gun in one hand in the 45 degree position discussed on page 000. This means that good modelling can be achieved and the shadow can fall further down behind the subject.

An alternative is to use bounce flash. In this technique you can

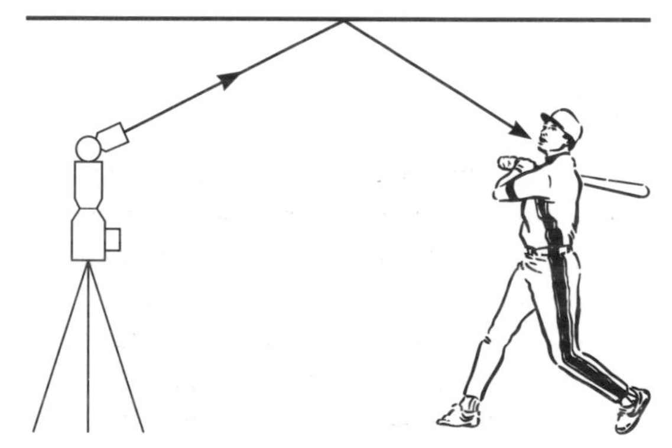

Fig. 8.3 Bounce flash.

Fig. 8.4 Portrait taken using diffused bounce flash. The whole effect is far more attractive than Figure 8.3.

bounce light from your flash unit off a reflecting surface. This can be the ceiling or a wall or even a piece of white cardboard. Figures 8.3 and 8.4 show how someone can be photographed using bounce flash off the ceiling.

This kind of flash gives nicely diffused lighting and the shadows are well reduced. Ensure, however, that the surface from which you bounce the flash is not coloured. If it is, a colour cast can be produced which may spoil a colour photograph. White surfaces are usually best.

With automatic flash guns which have a sensor in a fixed position, it is not possible to use bounce flash in automatic setting. This is because the flash unit will measure the correct exposure for the bounce surface, not the subject. These must be used on the manual setting. Some automatic units, however, have the facility for pointing the sensor at the subject regardless of which direction the electronic flash head is pointing. These units can be used on automatic setting for bounce flash.

For exposure calculations when using bounced flash, measure the distance from the flash to the ceiling and then from the ceiling to the subject. Add these two distances together and use the total distance to calculate your f/number using the guide number of the flash; then, to allow for light scattering, open up one extra stop.

## Studio electronic flash

Studio electronic flash lights are like studio incandescent lights in that they are usually fairly large units on stands and work off the mains power supply. Most are fitted with modelling lights which are low-wattage tungsten lamps that can be used to see the shadow effects that will be produced when the electronic flash unit is fired.

Studio electronic flash fitted with umbrellas is today a very popular form of lighting. Typically an arrangement might consist of a main or key light fitted with a reflective umbrella and the fill would use a more diffused umbrella. When a very diffused light source is needed, special studio electronic flash units consisting of very large areas of translucent material illuminated by flash tubes can be used.

Recently, because of revived interest in more directional studio lighting, electronic flash tubes fitted inside spotlight housings have become very popular. Just as in the case of incandescent light spotlights they produce very directional lighting.

## Exposure determination

Exposure with studio flash really has to be determined with a flash meter. Such meters usually measure the incident light on the subject. The meter is attached to the usual synchronising lead and a button is pressed on the meter to fire the flash and take a reading. The meter is positioned near the subject pointing towards the camera.

## Fill-in flash

Flash light can often be used as a supplement to daylight. It can be used to lighten shadows and in the case of against-the-light photography it can be used to lighten the shaded areas. Fill-in flash out of doors is sometimes called 'synchro-sunlight'. A good general rule for fill-in flash is that the flash exposure should be kept at one stop wider than whatever the correct exposure is for the daylight situation.

For example, if the correct daylight exposure was 1/125 s at f/11, then the flash used should be adjusted so that the 'correct' exposure given by the flash would be at f/8. This means that the shadows will be lightened but will not over-light the subject. If the flash exposure is equal to or greater than the daylight exposure, the picture can look very odd with the subject at first 'glowing' and the overall effect then becomes similar to a night shot. In other words, what is termed in the movie business a 'day-for-night' shot.

Since the fastest shutter speed for electronic flash synchronisation for focal plane shutters is often quite long, problems can arise when using electronic flash in sunlight. There are no such difficulties, of course, when using between-the-lens shutters. Synchro-sunlight using focal plane shutters and bulb flash is more feasible but does require careful calculation. This, however, is beyond the scope of our discussion here.

## Summary

**In this chapter we have described the characteristics of bulb and electronic flash photography. Exposure determination and use of both kinds of flash have been discussed. Studio electronic flash has also been covered. Techniques for using fill-in flash were described.**

# 9 Film Processing

At the end of this chapter you will know how a film is processed and, with suitable equipment, you will be able to develop a film for yourself.

## Cleanliness and safety

Good, careful and clean processing techniques are essential if you want to get good results – and stay healthy. These really are a matter of common sense.

All processing solutions should be regarded as harmful to you and, at the wrong times, to your work. Always keep your work area clean and clean up your equipment, tanks, dishes, measuring cylinders, bottles, etc., after use. Dried chemicals form dust which can fall on your film or paper, staining it or producing spots, or they can contaminate fresh solutions bringing about various problems.

Always work carefully and avoid contact of chemical solutions with skin and eyes and take care not to inhale fumes or dust. Do not store solutions in empty food or drink bottles for instance. Make a general rule to label everything most carefully.

In the event of accidentally drinking a solution or getting any in your eyes, seek immediate medical attention. Try to avoid all contact with solutions in printing by using tongs to pick up paper. Sometimes your hands may come in contact with some solution. In black and white photography this usually does not matter if you wash your hands as soon as possible. However, some people are sensitive to certain chemicals in developers – notably Metol. If you get a skin rash after using developers, you must see your doctor. In most black and white photography, the general run of chemicals are not exceptionally toxic; however, many used in colour photography and in toning techniques can be very poisonous and care should be taken at all times. When handling strong acids take exceptional care; wear gloves and goggles and in diluting such acids *always* add the concentrated acid very slowly *to* water and not the other way about.

Never *smoke* in the darkroom. This is not only a health warning, but smoke and ash can seriously damage your photographic work. Be warned!

Processing of black and white film involves a series of chemical reactions which converts the latent image on the film to a visible permanent negative image that can be used to make a print.

As we have seen in Chapter 4, the film emulsion is composed of minute crystals of silver halide suspended in gelatine. When light strikes the emulsion some of the silver halide is affected by light and some not. The development process is the conversion of those silver halide crystals affected by light to black metallic silver while those silver halides not affected by light remain unchanged. The familiar negative image is built up in which the bright areas of the image darken and the dark, or shadow, areas in the image remain virtually unaffected. This process is known as development.

In this chapter it is not proposed to discuss in detail the chemistry of the development process. It should be noted, however, that developers are mixtures of a number of chemicals. The main developing agents are organic-reducing agents, two common ones being metol and hydroquinone. Another substance in a typical developer is the accelerator, which is usually alkaline. This is used because the main developing agents need an alkaline medium to convert the silver halide to black metallic silver. Other chemicals often found in developers are preservatives such as sodium sulphite, which helps prevent the developer being oxidised by the oxygen in the air, and restrainers, which slow the developing process and minimise chemical fog.

Ideally, the development process should result in only those silver halide crystals that are affected by light being converted into metallic silver and all those unaffected by light remaining as silver halide. In practice, this is not quite the case. Some of the silver halide that is unaffected by light gets converted during the development process to metallic silver, and this results in a slight background density or 'fog'. The amount of this background fog depends on the properties of the film and developer being used.

When development has taken place, the developing chemicals are either kept for re-use or poured away and a rinse bath is used to stop development; it is then necessary to remove the silver halide that has not been affected by light. If this is not done, a fuzzy opaque image will result and, on exposure to light, the unaffected silver halide will eventually darken. Removal of the unaffected silver halide is done during the fixation process. The fixer or 'Hypo' is used to remove the unchanged silver halide. It does this by converting the insoluble silver halide in the emulsion into complex silver salts which are soluble in water.

Finally, the film is washed in water to remove all the residual chemicals and it is then hung up to dry.

Another developing agent which has been found to be most successful is p-aminophenol. This is the basis of the high dilution developer Agfa Rodinal.

All developing agents in common use today were discovered a hundred years ago. The only important new one is Phenidone, discovered in the Ilford laboratories in the 1940s. It can be used as a substitute for metol.

The formula below shows the make-up of one of the best-known film developers, Kodak D76. This is the same formula as Ilford ID11 and is one that has become accepted as a standard against which the performance of other developers are compared. As you will see, it contains metol and hydroquinone.

| D76 or ID11 | |
|---|---|
| Metol | 2 gm |
| Sodium sulphite (anhydrous) | 100 gm |
| Hydroquinone | 5 gm |
| Borax | 2 gm |
| Water | 1000 ml |

One reads of grain as fine as that produced by D76 or not as fine as D76 as the case may be. While the published formulae of D76 and ID11 are identical, it is said that the pre-packaged developers marketed by the two manufacturers are slightly different.

## Solutions for processing

There are five stages in processing black and white film. These are: development, wash or stop bath, fixation, washing and drying. The actual developer you use will depend on the kind of results that you require and what facilities you have for making up solutions.

## Development

You can make up your own developers from the basic chemicals. A very good book on the subject is *Developing* by C.I. and R.E. Jacobson, published by Focal Press.

Pre-packaged powder developers are obtainable and examples of these are Ilford ID11 and Kodak D76 (which we have already mentioned), Ilford Microphen and Kodak Microdol-X. Many of these packaged developers can be used several times. Development time need to be increased slightly for each film and full instructions are always given in the leaflet in the developer packet.

The number of films that can be developed in a given quantity of developer can be increased also by the use of so-called replenishers. When using replenishers, a little of the original developer is removed and replaced by replenisher solution. Many more films can be developed in this way before the solution is no longer usable.

There are also liquid concentrated developers. These are most convenient to use because they are simply diluted with water to make up a working strength solution. Usually such diluted developers are used only once and disposed of immediately after use. For this reason they are often called 'One-Shot' developers. Typical examples are Paterson Acutol, Agfa Rodinal and Kodak HC110.

### Review

**Developers are often classified as fine grain, semi-fine grain or acutance developers. Various claims are made by manufacturers and users of remarkably good results with this or that developer. Without disputing such claims, it can be stated that to a large extent the characteristics of the image are fixed by the kind of film you are using. A slow fine-grain film will tend to be rather contrasty and the grain pattern will be small. A fast film will tend to show rather more grain and will have less contrast. To some extent, the properties of the image will be influenced by the developer you use. But this influence occurs only to a limited extent. Developers such as Acutol and Rodinal, which are used in**

**high dilution, will show very sharp detail. However, the grain size is sometimes bigger than with developers such as Kodak D76. Very fine grain developers will sometimes reduce grain size but at the cost of reducing definition.**

## Wash or stop bath

When development is complete, it is necessary to stop further development quickly and to prevent carrying over developer from the film into the fixer. After development, the film can be rinsed in water or in a slightly acidic stop bath. A stop bath consists of a solution of a weak acid such as 2 per cent acetic and is sometimes stated to be more effective in stopping development than plain water. This is because developers work in an alkaline solution and if they are made acid they will no longer convert silver halide to metallic silver. For most work, however, a plain water rinse is quite sufficient.

## Fixation

As we have said earlier, before the negative can be exposed again to light, the undeveloped silver halides need to be removed thus making the image permanent and removing the milky veiling caused by the halides.

The most commonly used fixer is sodium thiosulphate (hypo). Sometimes a hardening agent is included with the hypo to harden the gelatine and make the film emulsion more resistant to scratching.

There are rapid fixers which, instead of sodium thiosulphate, contain ammonium thiosulphate. These are rather more expensive than plain hypo fixers but have the great advantage of working very rapidly indeed.

## Washing and drying

After fixation it is necessary to wash the film free of any remaining chemicals left behind from the other stages. If this is not done, staining or fading will occur. A final rinse in water with a few drops of wetting agent can be very helpful in preventing drying marks. After washing, the film is hung up to dry.

## Processing a film

The following is an outline of the stages in processing a film.

The equipment you need is quite simple and for film development you do not need a darkroom. Many readily available developing tanks need to be loaded in the dark, but as soon as the film is safely inside all the development processes can be carried out in the light.

Fig. 9.1 Developing tanks and film spirals available in a number of sizes from Paterson-Photax Ltd.

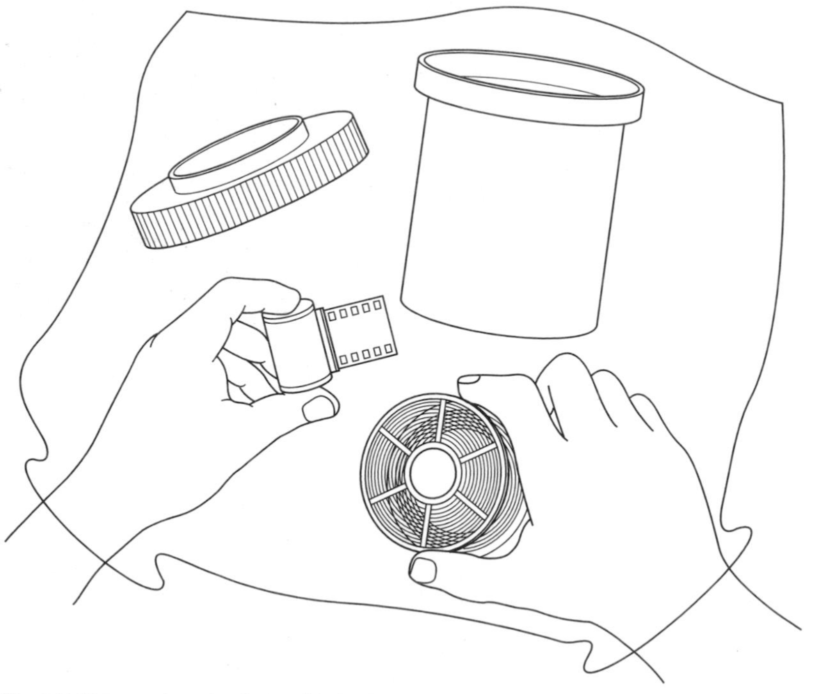

Fig. 9.2 Using a changing bag to load a film into a developing tank.

A developing tank (Figure 9.1) consists of a light-tight container designed in such a way as to let you pour solutions in and out without allowing any light to enter the tank. Inside there is a plastic, or sometimes metal, spiral into which you load the film. Spirals can be adjusted for different sizes of film and tanks are also made in various sizes so that from one to five films can be developed at the same time.

**Fig. 9.3** Film being washed while still on the spiral and inside the developing tank. (Photo: Paterson Products Ltd.)

## Changing bag

A changing bag is made of lightproof black cloth and it has two elasticated arm holes. There is also provision by a zip or buttons to put film spiral and parts of the developing tank inside the bag.

A changing bag (Figure 9.2) is a very useful accessory to have because not only can you load developing tanks in it, but if your camera should jam half-way through a film, you can open up your camera in perfect darkness to free the film or replace it.

If you do not have a changing bag, you can load your tank if you can find a suitable dark corner in your home, such as inside a wardrobe or under the bed clothes. Unless you are really confident that there is no light in your chosen location, wait until well after dark at night.

There are also available some developing tanks which can actually be loaded in daylight. One such is the Jobo 2400 Daylight Tank.

You will need a thermometer to measure the temperature of your solutions. You will also need at least two measuring cylinders for mixing your solution: one to measure quantities up to 1 litre and a smaller one for measuring up to 100 ml.

Two or three plastic beakers with a capacity of at least 1.5 litres are needed for mixing solutions, and plastic stirring rods will also be required.

At least one funnel will be needed, and a plastic hose for washing the film while still in the tank (Figure 9.3) is a most useful accessory.

You need film clips to hang up your film to dry, although clothes pegs work very well indeed. A clock or watch is a necessity, preferably giving you accurate countdown timings, but a stop watch or clock with a second hand will do.

You will need some storage containers of at least 1 litre capacity in which to store your solutions. Even if you are using one-shot developers, a container to store fixer is desirable because this can be used a number of times.

The first stage in developing a film is load your film into the spiral. If you are using a 35-mm film, cut off the leader end taking care that the cut is straight across and goes *between* the sprocket holes; if the leader is in the cassette, prise off the end of the cassette. This, of course, must be done in total darkness or in the changing bag. Then feed in the film from the cassette.

**There are various methods of loading the spiral and you should consult the instructions provided with your tank to make sure you know exactly what to do.**

It is a very good idea to practice loading the tank first of all with a dummy film in daylight before trying to do it in the dark. It is worth sacrificing a film to make sure that the first one you try is not ruined.

After the film is loaded into the spiral, put the spiral into the tank, close the lid and the tank can then be removed from the changing bag.

In the case of roll film, the film itself is attached to backing paper. In the dark you will need to unroll the film from the backing paper, detach it and then insert the film into the spiral.

## Developing

Three important variables must be controlled if you want reproducible results. These are **time**, **temperature** and **degree of agitation**.

### Time

In the instructions provided with your film or developer, you will see how long the manufacturer suggests that you should develop the film at 20 °C. You can develop at temperatures of a few degrees on either side of 20 °C, in which case the time of development has to be changed. Above 20 °C you must use a shorter development time; below 20 °C, a longer development time. Again the developer instructions will tell the adjustments you need to make. Tank development times should not normally be shorter than 5 minutes. It is very difficult to make sure that development in most tanks is even when developing for less than 5 minutes. Try to use, therefore, a film/developer combination which will give you a development time of 5 minutes or more.

### Time and temperature

It is recommended that most black and white films are developed at 20 °C. Make sure your developer is at this temperature by using your thermometer. It is important to keep the developer temperature reasonably constant during the development period. This can be done by allowing the tank to stand in a sink of warm water at 20 °C during the development process.

During fixation, agitation should take place every minute or so but it is by no means as important as it is during the development process. The time for fixation will depend on the fixer you use and the instructions should be consulted. After fixation, the developer should be returned to the storage bottle as it can be used a number of times. Again, the number of times that you can use the fixer will appear in the instructions.

### Agitation

To make sure that development is even, it is necessary to agitate the film in the developer. The way in which you agitate the film depends on the tank you use. Some have a rod to rotate the spiral in the developer. Many others have a watertight lid so you can invert the tank to agitate the solution. Generally the tank should be agitated for about 15 seconds once every minute.

The procedure is to pour the developer as quickly as possible into the developing tank. You will have made up the developer according to instructions and made sure that the volume you have ready to pour in is correct for the tank and the number of films you are developing and that it is at the correct temperature.

Commence timing as soon as you pour in the developer. As soon as the tank is full you should tap it two or three times on your table top to dislodge any air bubbles on the film and then agitate for 15 seconds. Put the tank down, and after 1 minute agitate it again. Repeat every minute until the development time is complete. At the end of the development time, pour out the developer quickly, drain the tank for a few seconds and then pour in either the stop bath or rinse water. Agitate again, and after about 15 seconds pour out the stop bath and immediately pour in the fixer.

### Washing

After fixation, you can remove the film from the tank but before taking it off the spiral it should be washed thoroughly. The easiest way to wash a film is shown in Figure 9.3. Let water run through the tank quite quickly.

It is important to keep the temperature of the solutions reasonably close. The rinse or stop bath and the fixer should be within about 4 to 5 °C of the temperature of the developer. In winter, washing water from the tap is likely to be very much colder than 20 °C, in fact it may be around 4 or 5 °C. If cooling is too fast, the gelatine on the film may be damaged, producing a pattern known as reticulation. Therefore, in winter, it is a good idea to reduce the

Fig. 9.4 The Paterson negative filing system in the foreground. Behind is shown the range of contact printing frames available. (Photo: Paterson-Photax Ltd.)

temperature of the film by two or three stages down to the same temperature as wash water, then there will be no trouble with reticulation. Washing should go on for about 30 to 40 minutes, although this time can be considerably shortened by using a special fast-washing device produced by some manufacturers of processing equipment.

After washing, add a few drops of wetting agent to the last tankful. Move the film spiral up and down to mix thoroughly and then hang up your film. The film should be hung up in a dust-free area to dry. Do not squeegee the film – even though this is recommended in some textbooks. Wet emulsion is delicate and small particles of dust and grit can cause marks on the film. When dry, the film should be cut into suitable lengths and stored in negative files. Several manufacturers produce filing systems in which strips of film can be stored and easily removed for printing. See Figure 9.4.

Figure 9.5 shows the various stages in processing a film. To get good results and to make sure those results are reproducible from one film to another, make sure that you follow exactly the same procedure each time, using the same temperatures, the same times and the same degree of agitation. Also make sure that you keep your equipment in thoroughly good order and, perhaps most important of all, keep it clean.

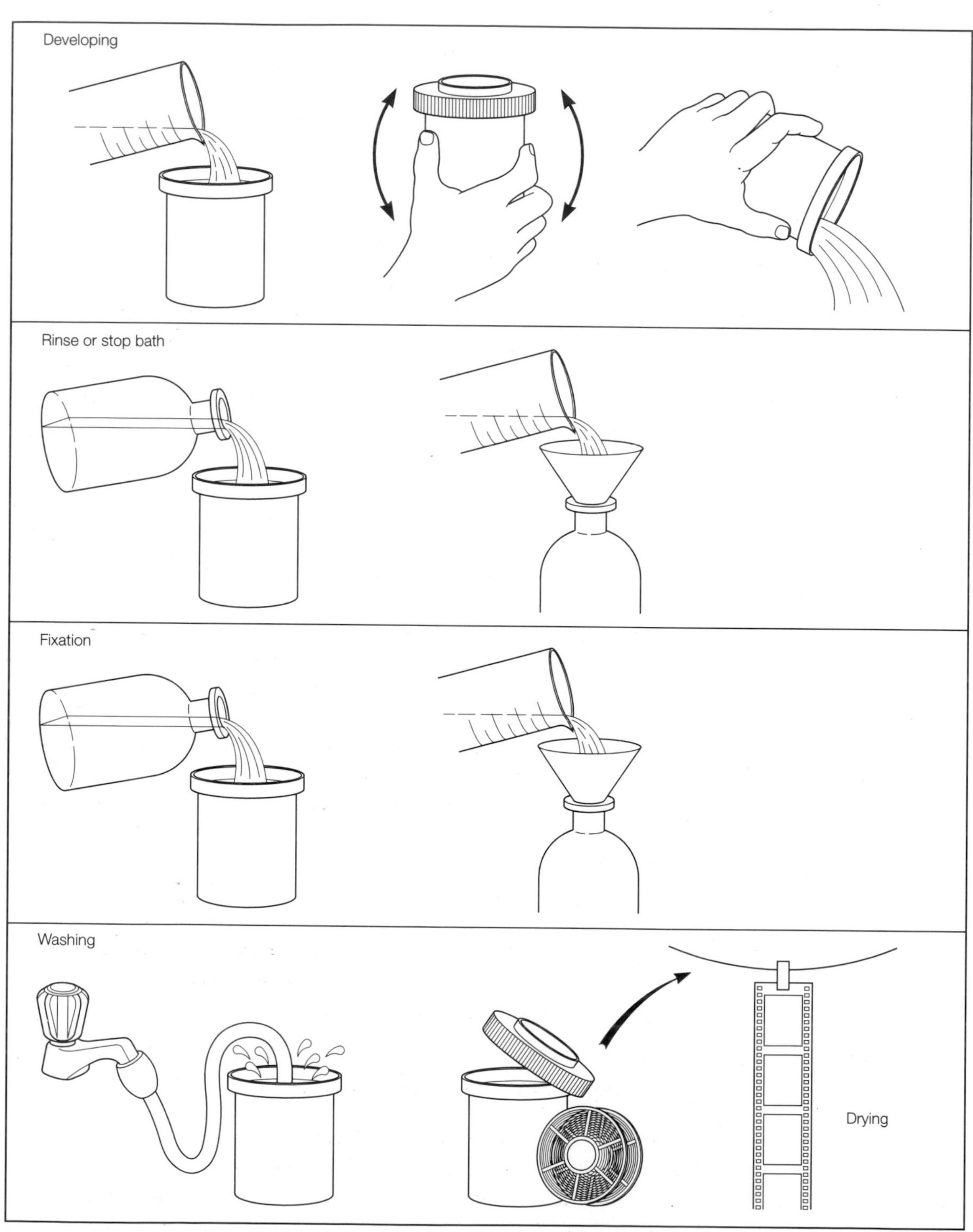


Fig. 9.5 Stages in processing a film.

## Faults in negatives

Some of the commoner faults in negatives can be very simply rectified. For example, if your negatives show tiny clear spots, which print as tiny black spots, they are very likely to have been caused by air bells. These are bubbles of air which have prevented the developer getting onto the film. The reason for the tap on the bench at the beginning of the development process is to remove such bubbles. If your water supply contains a lot of air, then air bubbles might occur. Usually a few extra taps on the tank at the beginning of development will dislodge them but sometimes it is necessary to add a few drops of wetting agent to the developer at the beginning.

Variations in the negative, particularly streaks extending down from the sprocket holes of 35-mm film, are likely to have been brought about by uneven development. To get rid of these, more frequent agitation is necessary.

Milky-looking negatives have not been fixed properly. If your negatives seem a bit opaque and have a distinctly milky sheen, the cause is almost certainly incomplete fixation. Perhaps your fixer was exhausted or the film was not long enough in the fixer. It is very simple to remove the milkiness by refixing your film.

If your negatives are quite clear, perhaps the film has not been exposed in the camera. If this has occurred, the manufacturer's name and a number will be visible on the edge of the film. If there is no name or numbering, then the film has not developed. This could have been due to fixing the film accidentally before development.

## Development time and exposure

The effective speed of a film and development time go hand in hand. If we give extra time in the developer, the film can be rated at a higher speed. This process is known as 'pushing' a film. While a film can be rated at a higher speed and given extra development time to compensate, it does become more grainy and more

Fig. 9.6 Negative normally exposed and normally developed.

Fig. 9.7 Negative under-exposed and over-developed.

Fig. 9.8 Negative over-exposed and over-developed.

Fig. 9.9 Negative under-exposed and under-developed.

Fig. 9.10 Negative over-exposed and under-developed.

contrasty. So a price is paid for extra speed. Conversely, under-development or a shorter development time will produce negatives that have much less contrast and need extra exposure. The various exposures and development of negatives can be compared in Figures 9.6 to 9.10.

These techniques are very useful in enabling the photographer to deal with very contrasty scenes or very flat scenes or take pictures under very low light conditions. An example would be where you need to double the ISO rating of a film because you are going to take pictures under very low light conditions of subjects that are not very contrasty.

A good rule is that every time you want to double the ISO rating, you increase the development time by 50 per cent. An ISO 400/27 film normally developed for 10 minutes will become an ISO 800/30 film if it is given 50 per cent more development time – that is, 15 minutes in all. The converse process is known as 'pulling'. If development time is decreased by 50 per cent, then the ISO speed is effectively halved.

## Exercise

Expose a film in your camera trying to make sure that your exposures are as uniform as possible – concentrate on average scenes and subjects. Choose a medium fine-grain developer such as D76 or Paterson Acutol. Process the film according to the instructions. When it is dry examine it carefully. Is it clean, unscratched and water-mark free? Is there full detail in the negatives and are they of reasonable contrast?

## Summary

**The processing of film has been discussed and instructions have been given for developing your own film. Pushing and pulling films has also been described.**

# 10 Printing and Enlarging

When you have finished this chapter, you will understand how to make contact prints and enlargements.

## The darkroom

In order to print and enlarge successfully, you do need darkroom facilities. There are, on the market, devices – such as the Pentax Daylab – which claim to enable you to make prints without a darkroom, but these items are somewhat cumbersome and difficult to use and are really only suitable as emergency stop gaps. They are only satisfactory if you are making a very small number of prints.

It is possible to convert a kitchen or bathroom into a suitable darkroom by using removable black-out material, and there are available some very ingenious fold-away darkrooms and even one which inflates like a rubber dinghy.

Basic equipment you will need to set up a darkroom are:

- enlarger and lens, fitted with, if possible, an exposure timer (see Figure 10.1)
- a safe-light
- contact printing frame
- a masking frame
- four dishes: one for developer, one for stop bath, one for fixer and, finally, one for storing prints prior to washing
- at least two pairs of print tongs
- at least three storage bottles for chemicals
- one good quality soft artist's brush

Also needed will be some of the items used in black and white developing (Figure 10.2), such as a thermometer, measuring cylinders, etc.

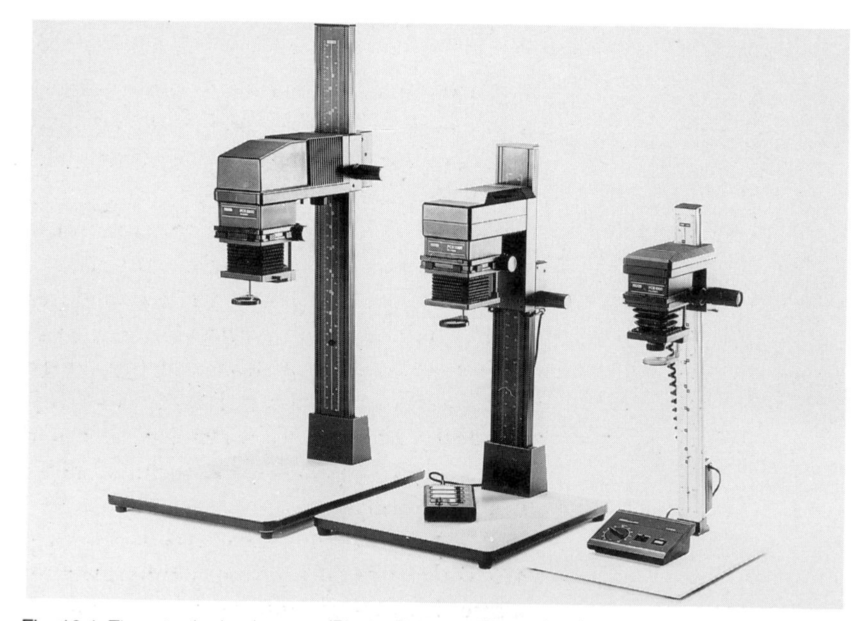

Fig. 10.1 Three typical enlargers. (Photo: Paterson-Photax Ltd.)

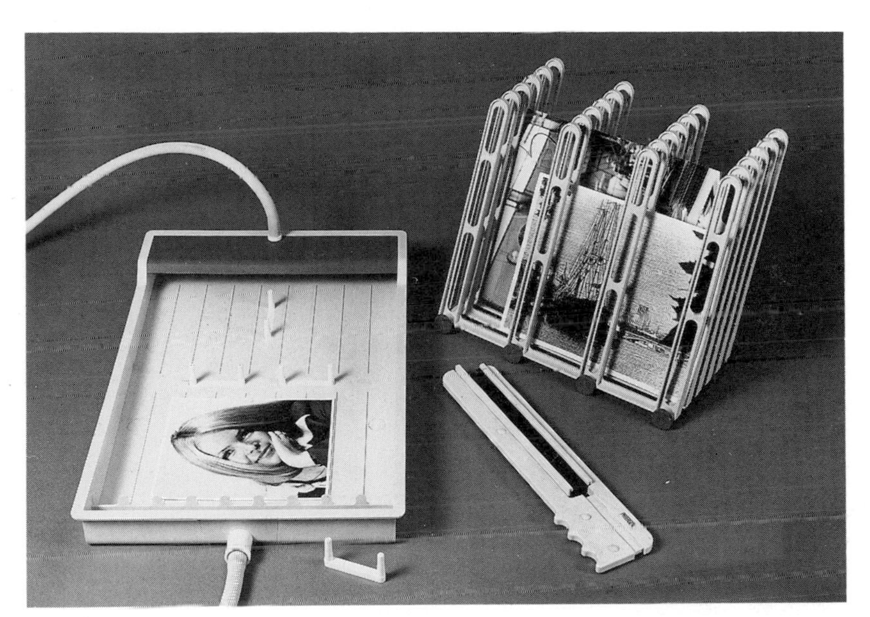

Fig. 10.2 A Paterson print washer (left); a Paterson print drying rack (right); and, in the foreground, a Paterson print squeegee for use with RC papers. (Photo: Paterson-Photax Ltd.)

**Caution**: whatever set-up you use, make sure it is adequately ventilated and be absolutely certain that any electrical equipment you use near a water supply is safely earthed. Preferably use a safety circuit breaker.

Best of all is to have a permanent darkroom set up but this, of course, is not always possible. If you are a student at college, you probably already have darkroom facilities available. If so, the next section will not be of particular interest to you.

A good darkroom should be light tight. A good test for a darkroom is to turn off all lights and stay in it for about 10 minutes to allow your eyes to become accustomed to the dark. If, at the end of that time, you can see any chinks of light, then the darkroom is not really safe.

A safe-light allowing you to see what you are doing is essential. A safe-light is usually a box or tube containing a low-wattage bulb and a filter is often provided – usually amber – which will not fog your printing paper. Some safe-lights, however, are safer than others.

It is worth while testing to make sure the safe-light you are using is not causing a background fog on your papers. The easiest way of doing this is to expose a sheet of enlarging paper on your bench with just the safe-light on. The safe-light should be at its usual working distance from your bench. Place a coin on the surface of the paper and expose it to the safe-light for a period of 10 minutes. Remove the coin and then develop the paper and fix it.

When you turn on your safe-light, you should not be able to discern an *outline* of the coin at all. If the safe-light was not safe, then the area around the coin will have produced a slight density while the area protected by the coin will have no such fogging. In some recent texts and articles, suggestions are made that with shorter processing times of the latest printing papers, it is adequate to test the safe-light for 1 to 2 minutes only. This is nonsense, because an unsafe safe-light may not produce any noticeable fogging of the paper in the time but will, nevertheless, degrade the image to a greater or lesser extent and so reduce image contrast and quality.

## Printing paper

Making a print is fundamentally the same process as making a negative. Printing paper has a silver halide emulsion just as film does. The paper backing provides a support for the emulsion and provides us with a reflective surface so that we can view the image formed, as usual, with silver grains. As you will remember, the negative consists of an image in which the tones are reversed, the lightest areas in the original scene are dark and the darkest areas light. If we re-photograph the negative, the reverse takes place and again the dark parts of the negative appear light on the print and the light parts appear dark. This means that the tones of the original scene are reproduced correctly. **This is the basis of the printing process.**

There are two kinds of printing paper available at present. These are contact printing papers and enlarging papers. Contact printing paper is very much slower than enlarging papers. At one time it was very common but is quite rare today, at least in Britain. At one time contact prints were made in small printing frames directly from negatives and, as the negatives were quite large, such prints were quite satisfactory for most people. Contact prints were exposed using ordinary household lights and so the darkroom facilities were very simple. Enlarging paper is much faster and so needs much less illumination. Light from an enlarger is ideal for making contact prints with enlarging paper. We shall see how this is done later.

Enlarging papers are themselves divided into a number of different categories. The two main types are 'RC' or resin-coated papers and 'fibre-based' papers. RC papers use a plastic-coated paper as the carrier for the emulsion, whereas fibre-based papers use a standard paper base. The most significant difference between these two types of paper is that solutions do not penetrate the RC base, thus processing is quicker and washing is very much quicker. RC papers also tend to dry flat.

Fibre-based papers, on the other hand, absorb solutions, are slower to process and washing takes much longer. It is claimed by many photographers, however, that fibre-based papers give a higher quality image. With the development of improved emulsions, it could, perhaps, be argued that this is no longer true. As with many other artistic matters, such things can often be decided only by personal taste. RC papers are certainly easier to handle and it is recommended that the beginner use these at first.

Printing papers are available in a wide variety of surfaces: glossy, matt, stipple, silk and so on. Again, the surface you use will depend on personal taste, but it is worth noting here that glossy paper is usually preferred by publishers of newspapers and magazines because it is easier to make reproductions from such prints.

Printing papers come in a wide variety of sizes and packaging. Sizes range from postcard and smaller (3½ × 5½ in., 5 × 7 in., 8½ × 6½ in., 8 × 10 in. and larger). 8 × 10 in. is a commonly used standard size. Packages are usually in 10s, 25s, 50s or 100s. It is always cheaper to buy the larger boxes.

## Paper grades

A good-quality black and white print will usually have, somewhere, a shadow area rendered as maximum black. Somewhere there will be a bright highlight recorded as pure white, and there will be a good range of tones in between. All significant areas in the picture will show detail.

To achieve this result, it is important that the contrast of the paper is correctly matched to the contrast of the negative.

A contrasty negative – that is, a negative with large differences in density between the darkest and lightest parts – will need a paper of low contrast to give a satisfactory print. A soft negative – that is, a negative with much less difference between the light and dark areas – will need a more contrasty paper to give a satisfactory result. A normal negative – that is, a negative with an average range of contrast – will give satisfactory prints when printed on 'normal' paper.

The contrast of paper is usually described by a series of numbers, usually between 0 and 5. The lower numbers 0, 1 and sometimes 2, are the lower contrast papers. Grades 2, and sometimes 3, are 'normal' papers and higher numbers are high-contrast papers. The higher the number, the greater the contrast. Actual degrees of contrast and their corresponding numbers vary between manufacturers.

The papers we have described above are fixed contrast papers. They will give the same degree of contrast each time, although some variations are possible using different types of developer. A photographer needs to have in stock supplies of, at least, grades 1, 2, 3 and possibly 4. This will cover most negatives, but for some difficult subjects very soft paper or very contrasty paper may be needed.

There are, however, papers available of **variable contrast**. These papers work by changing the colour of the light from the enlarger to change the contrast. This can be done by using appropriate filter combinations. The pioneer of variable contrast papers was **Ilford Multigrade**.

For many years the excellent Kodak Polycontrast papers were available only in the United States. Now they are on sale in Britain and are available as Polycontrast and Polyprint papers.

A relative newcomer in the field but possibly providing the best quality of all are Agfa Multicontrast papers. Very recently a number of other manufacturers have put variable contrast papers on the market. The great advantage of these papers is that you only need to keep one box in stock and the contrast of the paper is controlled by the filters you use. Full instructions are provided for these papers in the leaflet in their boxes. Also, the manufacturers' booklets on how to get the best results from their products should always be consulted.

## Processing chemicals for paper

Processing printing paper is essentially the same as processing black and white negatives. A developer is required, a stop bath or rinse and a fixer.

### Developers

Print developers work in basically the same way as negative developers. Their chemical make-up, however, is different. Film developers cannot be used for developing prints. If they are used, by mistake, you will find that the resulting prints are very grey and flat. Print developers are faster acting and more contrasty than negative developers, so if you use these for developing your films, development times will be very short and most contrasty results will be obtained. You should keep to the appropriate developer for the particular job.

Some so-called 'Universal' developers are available. Different dilutions of these developers are suggested for papers and for films, but they are a compromise and are not recommended.

### Fixers

The fixer you use for developing your films can also be used for fixing your papers. Standard fixer is sodium thiosulphate while the rapid variety contains ammonium thiosulphate. Some manufacturers suggest different dilutions for papers and for films. Again, check the manufacturer's instructions before making up your solutions. It is generally considered unnecessary to use a hardener in your fixer. However, you should always keep separate solutions of the fixer you use for films and the fixer you use for papers.

**Life of solutions**

Very roughly, it can be said that a litre of print developer will probably process about thirty 8 × 10 in. prints. A litre of standard fixer will probably do for about the same number. The rapid fixers, however, will fix more prints; a litre being safe for about fifty 8 × 10 in. prints.

Print developers are usually made up from concentrated solutions. The working strength solution does not keep well so should be thrown out after a printing session. The fixer, if the number of prints fixed has not reached the maximum, can be kept and used again.

> Sensitive material and chemicals should always be kept separate. Try, therefore, to arrange your darkroom or darkroom space so that there is a wet bench and a dry bench. On the dry bench you should keep your enlarger, printing paper and negatives. Make it a rule never to put solutions, developing tanks, measuring cylinders or wet negatives or paper on the dry bench. On the wet bench all the solutions, tanks and processing trays should be placed. Arrange each bench so that the flow of work goes logically across it. For instance, it is a good plan to work from left to right, so arrange the processing trays, from left to right, in the order: developer, rinse/stop and fixer. You can use a fourth dish containing water on the right to hold fixed prints waiting to be washed. Such a routine will help you to avoid errors such as putting a print in the fixer before it has been developed. Your college darkroom or your own preference may dictate that you work from right to left. This does not really matter as long as you establish one routine and keep to it.

## Contact printing

Contact printing is actually putting the negative to be printed in contact with the sensitive surface of the printing paper. You then shine a light through the negative to expose the paper, and process it.

The quickest and easiest way to become familiar with the various steps in contact printing and in processing paper is to make a few

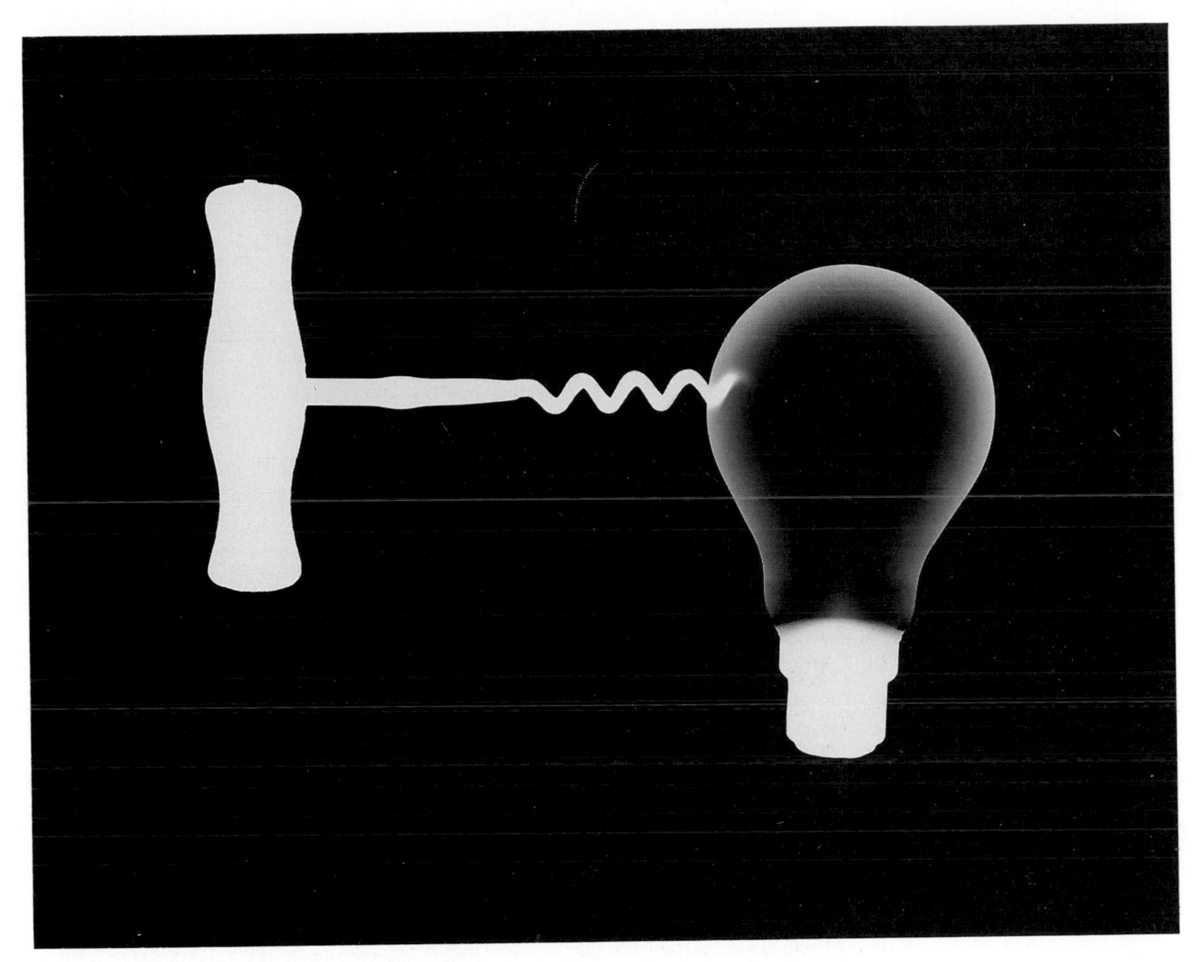

Fig. 10.3 A photogram. (Photo: Barbara Egervary.)

photograms. To make a photogram, first raise your enlarger to a moderate height, making sure that the beam of light from the enlarger covers a little more than the masking frame and the piece of paper you propose to use. Stop down the enlarger lens to a medium aperture. Turn off the white light in the darkroom and put a piece of enlarging paper in the masking frame.

A photogram (Figure 10.3) is really a silhouette print of any small object. You can use a feather, a fir cone, a developing tank spiral, some beads or pieces of paper. What will happen when you turn on the enlarger light is that the areas not covered by objects will be exposed and will turn black on development and the white silhouettes of the objects will remain. Very attractive results can be had using translucent or semi-translucent objects such as a developing spiral or an electric light bulb. Exposure is not critical and satisfactory results will be obtained over quite a wide range of exposures.

After the exposure had been made, the paper should be processed. The way to do this is to slide the paper quickly under the surface of the developer in the tray, emulsion side up. The tray should be rocked gently during the development process and you will find that the image commences to appear very soon after putting it in the developer. This may occur after 10 to 15 seconds in the case of RC papers but sometimes a little over 30 seconds in the case of fibre-based papers. Usually development is complete in about 1 minute for RC papers or 2 minutes for fibre-based papers. After development, the print should be carefully lifted out of the developer using print tongs, allowed to drain, transferred into the rinse dish, moved about a little and then transferred into the fixer.

After about 20 seconds in the fixer you can turn on the white light and examine the result. Before turning on the light always make sure that the printing paper box has been closed and that no unexposed printing paper is likely to be exposed to light and so ruined. A very good investment are the so-called 'paper safes' which allow you to take out one sheet only at a time and keep the rest safe from accidental exposure.

If you are using ordinary fixer, the prints must remain in the fixer dish for about 10 minutes (rapid-fix requires only 2 minutes) and should be moved about from time to time. This is very important when several prints are in the fixer to make sure that they do not stick together and so prevent the solution reaching the emulsion surface of any of them. After fixation, the prints should be washed in running water. In the case of RC papers, 10 minutes' washing is perfectly sufficient. However, fibre-based papers need about 1 hour's washing in running water to make sure that all the chemicals are removed. After washing, prints should be dried, and drying racks are a very useful accessory. Prints can be stacked in these and allowed to dry. Very much more expensive are electric dryers. However, if you are making large numbers of prints regularly, it

Fig. 10.4 Contact printing frames suitable for both 35-mm and 120-mm negatives. (Photo: Paterson-Photax Ltd.)

may well be worth while investing in one of these. A good electric dryer will dry RC papers in a matter of minutes.

## Contact prints

Contact prints are made in exactly the same way as photograms. Here you place your negatives directly in contact with the printing paper. Printing frames or proof printers are available which will enable you to do this.

In making contact prints of 35-mm negatives, for example, you will find that a standard 36 exposure 35-mm film will cut up into six strips of six negatives. These strips can be accommodated on an 8 × 10 in. sheet of printing paper. Most contact printing frames have a means of holding the negative and the bromide paper in contact. Such equipment is shown in Figure 10.4. The same kind of illumination that was used to make a photogram can be employed to make contact prints. It is, however, important to estimate the exposure more accurately. This can be done by making a test strip.

## Exercise

A test strip can be made by loading the printing frame with a strip of paper about 2 in. wide and 6 or 7 in. long. The emulsion side of the paper should, of course, face upwards. Arrange the strip so that it covers several strips of your negatives. Close the frame and place it under the enlarger. Before turning on the enlarger, cover all but about 1 in. of the paper strip with a piece of black card. Then switch on the enlarger for 5 seconds. Move the card to uncover another inch and expose again for 5 seconds. The first inch will then have had 10 seconds' exposure and the second inch 5 seconds. If you now move the card again and give another 5 seconds' exposure, the first inch will have had 15 seconds, the second inch 10 seconds and the third inch 5 seconds. Continue this process until you have uncovered all the paper strip. When this has been done, develop the paper giving it a full development of about 1½ minutes. Rinse the paper and put it in the fixer. After a short time turn on the white light and have a look at the result. If your test strip contains a good range of tones varying from quite light to quite dark, you can choose the exposure that looks best and then use this to expose the full set of negatives using a full-size piece of paper. If all the test strip is too dark, it has been over-exposed. In this case close down the lens aperture by a couple of stops and try the process again. If all the test strip is too light, it has been under-exposed so open up the aperture by a couple of stops and try again. The final print is washed and dried in the usual way.

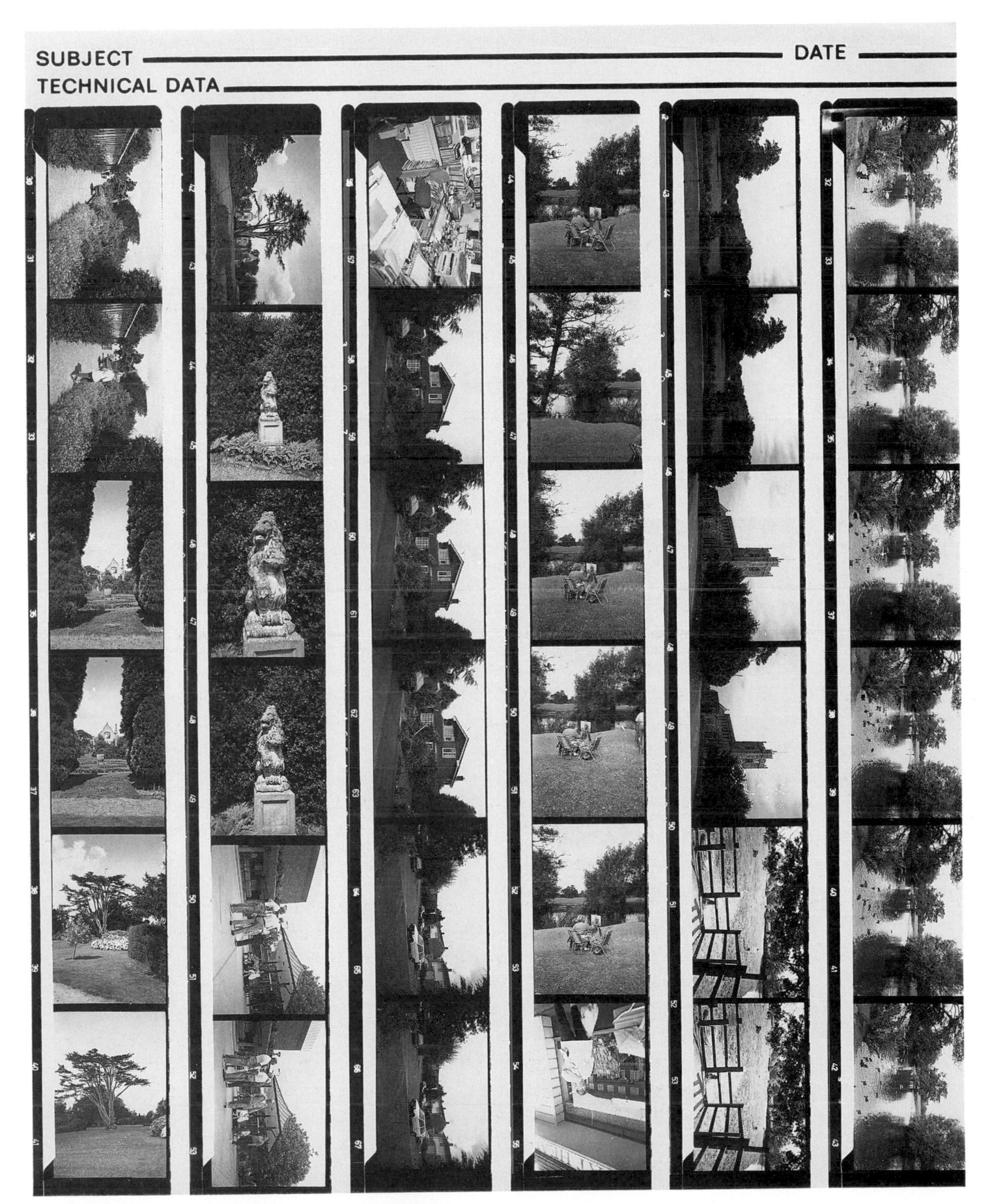


Fig. 10.5 Contact print sheet made from a 35-mm film.

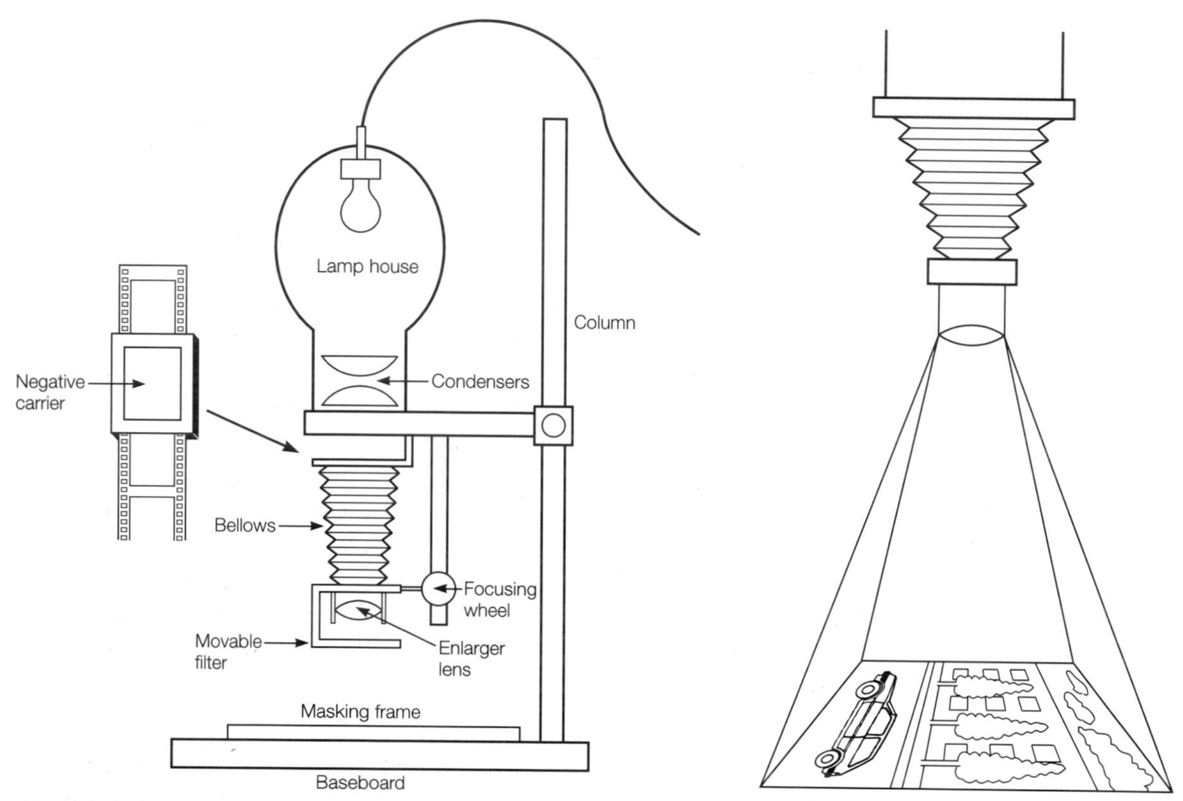


Fig. 10.6 An enlarger.

Fig. 10.7 Print being made under the enlarger.

Contact sheets of sets of negatives are very valuable because they give you an easy means of evaluating your pictures without making an enlargement. Even contact sheets from 35-mm negatives can be examined with a magnifying glass for fine detail. Contact prints can be marked up to show the areas you would like to enlarge later and are very useful for filing purposes. It is very difficult indeed to evaluate negatives, and contact prints of your negatives are really a necessity. A full 35-mm film in strips of six can be printed on an 8 × 10 in. piece of paper and a 120 film can also be accommodated on an 8 × 10 in. sheet of paper in four strips. Figure 10.5 shows a typical set of 35-mm contact prints.

## Enlarging

When you have finished this section you will be able to make a satisfactory enlarged print from a negative on a suitable grade of paper.

## The enlarger

The enlarger is really a projector. It is used to project an image of the negative onto an easel holding the printing paper. Formerly, enlargers were very much like slide projectors. They were on their side and were used in the horizontal position. Today, enlargers are arranged so that they project vertically downwards and can be used conveniently at a bench height. Figure 10.6 shows a diagram of a typical simple enlarger.

Enlargers can be used for black and white printing only or they can be colour enlargers. Colour enlargers have a means of changing the colour of the light by using a pack of filters or by using a 'colour' head in which the colour of the light is changed. Colour head enlargers are useful in black and white printing when using variable contrast papers.

Enlargers are also classified depending on their optical system. There are condenser enlargers and diffuser enlargers. Condenser enlargers employ optical condenser lenses to collect the light from the enlarger bulb and direct it through the negative. Diffuser enlargers have a large diffused light source above the negative. Enlargers that use colour heads are usually diffuser enlargers. The main difference between the two systems is that condenser enlargers can produce more contrasty prints from black and white negatives than diffuser enlargers.

When using a condenser enlarger, grain in the negative will be reproduced more clearly and blemishes and dust tend to show up more in the prints. With a diffuser enlarger you may find you need to use harder grades of paper.

As you will see, an enlarger basically consists of a light source, an optical system to direct the light through the negative and a lens to focus the image of the negative on to a sheet of enlarging paper held in the masking frame. If the head of the enlarger is raised, the size of the image on the base board frame increases, if it is lowered, the size gets smaller. This lets the photographer not only decide on the size of the print required, but also the areas of the print that can be retained or excluded. Leaving out parts of the print is known as 'cropping'. Focusing is carried out by moving the lens further from or nearer to the negative. The aperture on the enlarger lens will, just like the aperture in the camera lens, affect exposure, depth of field and depth of focus.

In practice, the main function of the aperture in an enlarging lens is to help control exposure. Exposure time in enlarging can be controlled simply by switching the light on or off, but enlarger timers are very useful accessories. Exposure times can be pre-set to expose the print correctly at the touch of a button. Most timers have a manual override so that the enlarger lamp can be switched on for composing the print and focusing.

**Fig. 10.8** A typical test strip made in steps, as described in the text.

## Making an enlargement

First, select a good sharp negative of average contrast and place it in the negative carrier of the enlarger. The negative should be placed upside down in the carrier – that is, with the top of the positive facing the photographer. Make sure that, as in contact printing, the emulsion side of the negative is facing downwards and the emulsion of the paper facing upwards. A good rule to remember in printing is that *emulsion always faces emulsion* (unless, of course, you wish to reverse the negative and make a *mirror* image). Before placing the negative in the negative carrier, make sure that it is clean and dust free. Dust on the negative will appear as white spots on the print. Get into the habit of dusting off your negatives with a good quality artist's brush immediately before printing. With the negative in the carrier, open the lens to its maximum aperture with the masking frame below the enlarger lens and turn on the white light. Next, compose your picture by moving the enlarger up and down until the picture you require fills the area of the masking frame (Figure 10.7). You will need to focus the image roughly as you do this because you will soon find that focusing the image also changes its size a little.

To achieve final correct focus you may need one of the many focusing aids available. Some of these allow you to focus directly on the grain of the image.

Next, close down the lens aperture two or three stops and make a test strip. Use a normal grade of paper for your first try. The test strip should cover the most significant areas of your picture. Do not include too much sky. If possible, the area chosen should include both highlights and shadows. Next, expose inch sections of the strip just as you did with the contact print. Develop your test strip as usual (Figure 10.8).

When the test strip has been fixed and rinsed, examine it in white light and choose the exposure that looks best (Figure 10.9). You can

Fig. 10.9 Print made after assessing the test strip shown in Figure 10.8. Step 4 from the left was chosen as the correct exposure.

also use the test strip to decide which paper grade you use. If the test strip looks grey, use a harder grade of paper. If it looks too contrasty, choose a softer grade of paper. If it looks satisfactory, then the normal grade of paper should work.

We have already discussed to some extent how to match negative to an appropriate paper grade. Table 10.1 takes this a little further. However, practice really is the only thing to familiarise you with all the procedures that go to make a good print. Remember that a good print somewhere contains a maximum black, somewhere contains pure white and has good detail in all the tones in between.

Table 10.1 Matching negative characteristics to grade of printing paper

| Type of negative | Grade of paper to use |
|---|---|
| Under-exposed and under-developed | Very hard |
| Normally exposed but under-developed | Hard paper |
| Over-exposed but under-developed | Hard paper |
| Under-exposed and normally developed | Normal paper |
| Normally exposed and normally developed | Normal paper |
| Over-exposed and normally developed | Normal paper |
| Under-exposed and over-developed | Soft paper |
| Normally exposed and over-developed | Soft paper |
| Over-exposed and over-developed | Very soft paper |

## Local control

Occasionally a straight print will not give you best results. A better print can be obtained if, for example, extra time is given under the enlarger for specific areas, or perhaps less exposure is necessary in specific areas. The processes of giving more exposure or less exposure in specific areas of the print are known as **burning in** or **holding back**.

### Burning in

As we have said, burning in means giving more exposure to those areas of the picture that might otherwise look too light. A good example is a landscape in which the sky appears too bright. Extra exposure can darken the sky and even bring out clouds which are on the negative but do not appear in a straightforward print. The way that extra exposure can be given to the sky is to give extra time to the print while shading the foreground by a piece of card or with your hand. The card should be kept an inch or two above the print and should be moved gently backwards and forwards across the horizon line to prevent the appearance of a hard-edged shadow.

The original test strip can be used to give you an idea of the extra exposure required, but at first you will need to try two or three experimental prints before you can get it right. When burning in is done correctly, it is not possible to see where the two exposures merge. Figure 10.10 shows burning in being carried out and Figures 10.11 and 10.12 show a picture before and after burning in.

Sometimes only a very small area needs to be burned in. In a portrait, it may be necessary to subdue a bright area on a shoulder, for instance. This can be done simply by cutting a hole in a small piece of black card and after you have given the whole print its basic exposure, hold the card between the lens and the paper so that the bright area is projected through the hole (Figure 10.13). Move the card slowly in a circle so that a sharp shadow is not allowed to form.

Local burning in is a very useful way of reducing bright

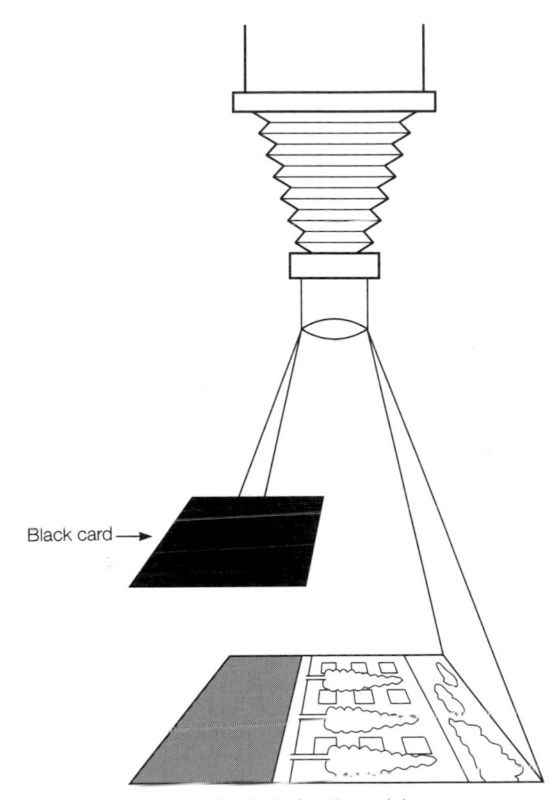

Fig. 10.10 Top part of print being 'burnt in'.

Fig. 10.11 Original picture before burning in. (Photo: Keith Hawkins.)

Fig. 10.12 Picture after burning in at the top. (Photo: Keith Hawkins.)

distracting detail in a photograph. As with other aspects of enlarging, plenty of practice is needed.

## Holding back

Holding back is the exact opposite of burning in. If it is found that shadow areas on a negative have detail, but in a correctly exposed print those shadows have recorded as dead black, then you can give the shadows less exposure. In order to do this, the area in question needs to be masked from the printing paper for part of the overall exposure. A small piece of card on the end of a wire can be used to do this and again it should be moved slowly during exposure (Figure 10.14). The results of 'holding back' can be seen by comparing Figures 10.15 and 10.16.

## Making a vignette

A vignetted portrait or a vignetted scene is attractive. In vignettes, the subject appears in an oval or circular shape and the print on the edges fades out to pure white. They are produced by the process of holding edges back. A suitable sized piece of black card with an oval or circle cut out can be used during the print exposure and, of course, it should be moved during exposure.

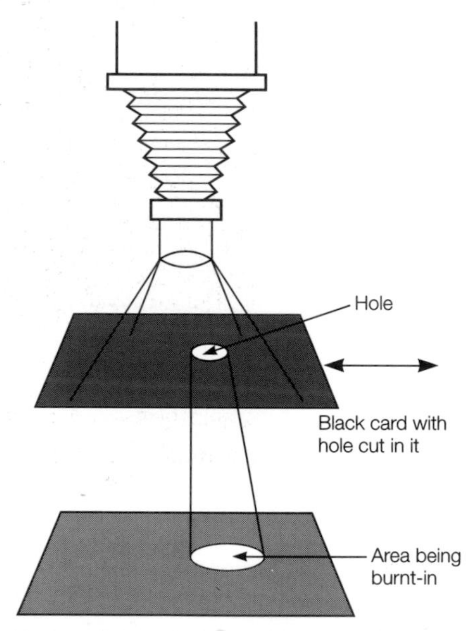


Fig. 10.13 Local burning in.

## Afterwork

Presentation of prints can be quite important and there is a certain amount of afterwork which makes your work look professional. The first of these is trimming. It is generally accepted that most prints should either have no margins or have margins that are equal. This can be done easily if you have a print trimmer.

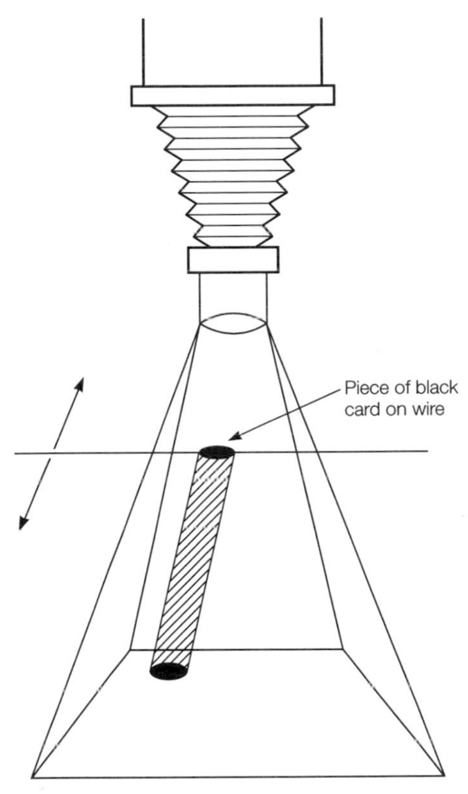


Fig. 10.14 Local holding back.

Fig. 10.15 Original picture before holding back. (Photo: Keith Hawkins.)

Fig. 10.16 Picture after holding back at the top. (Photo: Keith Hawkins.)

Spotting is also necessary. If white spots have appeared on the print they should be removed. Spotting is done by applying small areas of dye to the print with a fine brush. Spotting kits, provided with full instructions for use, are available and are quite inexpensive.

A mounted print looks very good and is quite easy to do. Good-quality mounting board should be used. There are various methods of sticking your prints down to the mounting board but you must be careful not to use ordinary glues. A specially manufactured spray adhesive for mounting photographs is probably best. Again, full instructions are provided with spray cans.

**Warning:** if you do use spray adhesive, use it only in a very well-ventilated area and avoid inhaling the spray.

## Toning

Toning is changing the colour of the photographic image. Sepia toning is probably the most common. In this technique a brown image is produced, but today there are other methods available for producing a very wide range of tones and colours. For further reading we suggest below a number of references to the technique of toning as well as more advanced enlarging techniques.

### Further Reading

*Leica Darkroom Practice* by Rudolph Seck, published by Hove Foto Books.

*The Complete Art of Printing and Enlarging* by O.R. Croy, published by Focal Press.

*Monochrome Darkroom Practice* by Jack H. Coote, published by Focal Press.

## Summary

**In this chapter we have discussed contact printing and enlarging and have given details of some of the more advanced techniques such as burning in and holding back.**

---

# 11 Colour Photography

When you have finished this chapter, you will understand how we perceive colour and how colour photography works. You will also understand how to take good colour photographs. However, before we can understand how colour photography works, we need to know something of visible light and the colours we see.

## Light

Visible light is actually only a very small part of natural electromagnetic radiation. Perhaps the easiest way of visualising electromagnetic radiation is to think about it as a means of transferring energy by wave motion. All wave motions have wavelengths. It is these wavelengths which determine the nature of radiation. Figure 11.1 shows the electromagnetic spectrum.

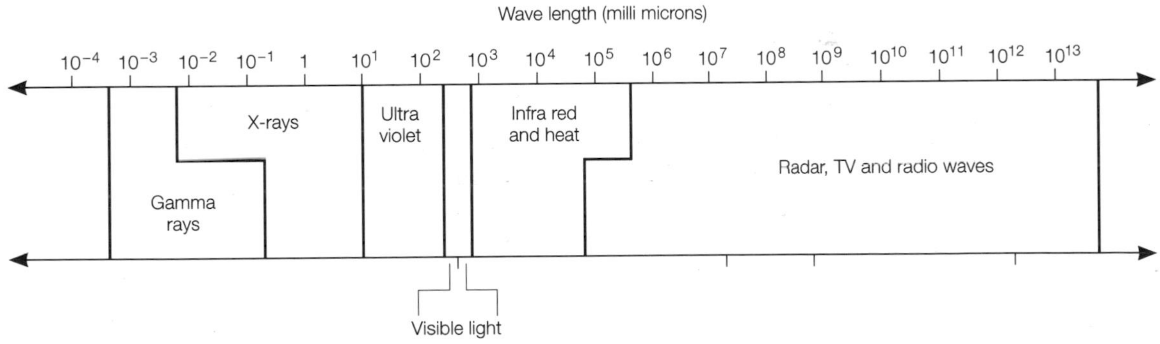


Fig. 11.1 The electromagnetic spectrum.

As you will see, electromagnetic radiation extends from cosmic and gamma rays at the short wavelength end to radio waves at the long end. Such wavelengths vary from minute fractions of a millimetre to over a mile.

Figure 11.1 shows that the section of the spectrum which we know as visible light is a small fraction sandwiched between ultraviolet radiation on the one hand and infrared and heat radiation on the other. Visible light has wavelengths between 400 and 700 nanometres. It is this section of the electromagnetic spectrum which stimulates our eyes and which we perceive as visible light.

The light-sensitive part of our eyes is called the **retina**. This contains two types of light-sensitive cells called **rods** and **cones**. The rods and cones, which are called **receptors**, are connected via nerves to the brain.

The rods that are found in greatest numbers are not found in the centre of the retina, but increase in numbers outwards from the centre. Although they are light-sensitive, they distinguish only between light and dark. They interpret shape, movement, texture, etc., are very sensitive, and react to very small amounts of light which enables us to see in very dim light.

The cones need a much higher intensity of light to activate them and that is why we do not see colours in dim light. However, in dim light we can see movement out of the corner of our eyes much better than in the centre of our visual field.

In the centre of the retina are the cones, which are sensitive only to certain restricted wavelengths of the visual spectrum. One group responds to light from the red end of the spectrum, a second group to the middle portion of the spectrum (mainly green) and a third group is sensitive to the blue light part of the spectrum.

The activated rods and cones send their messages to the brain via the optic nerve and it is, in fact, the interpretation of those messages by our brain which gives us the sensation we know as **colour**.

## Review

**From all this you will realise that colour is really a subjective sensation which we experience in our minds and is not a built-in property of an object like texture.**

For us to perceive colour, the intensity of the light must be above the threshold of colour perception. There must be an object to reflect light. If it is not white, grey or black, it means that it has the special property of selecting only a particular part of the spectrum of the light falling upon it.

There must also be an eye to receive and register the light from the object and there must be a brain behind the eye to interpret the message.

## The trichromatic theory of vision

When our eyes receive light which contains the complete range of wavelengths of visible light, our brain tells us that the light is white. That means that we perceive no colour in that light. If, however, the wavelengths in white light are spread out, we perceive a series of colours.

When sunlight passes through spherical raindrops we see a rainbow. Or, if we pass a beam of white light through a prism, a spectrum is produced. The colours of the spectrum, and of course a rainbow, and the order in which they appear, are **red, yellow, green, blue–green, blue, violet.** The colours appear to overlap and merge into one another. White light appears to us as white and to have no colour because it is a balanced mixture of all the colours of the spectrum.

Our eyes can mislead us and we can think that light is white when, in fact, its colour can vary over a wide range. Daylight is somewhat bluish and electric light in our homes is quite red. Both appear pure white to us and it can sometimes be a shock to look in a window of a house in the evening near twilight and see how red the electric lights look from the outside. As soon as we are inside, our eyes adapt and we automatically make a correction so that the light looks white to us. This fact is very important in relation to colour photography because colour emulsions cannot adapt to different colours of light.

### Review

**As we have described above, the trichromatic theory of vision tells us that there are three receptors in our eyes, one of which is receptive to red light, one to green light and the third one to blue light.**

When all three receptors are equally stimulated, the sensation is one of white light. When any one group of receptors is stimulated, we see either red, or green or blue light. However, as everyone knows, we see an enormous range of different colours in nature. The trichromatic theory of colour assumes that the other colours that we perceive are made up of a mixture of the three basic colours, and that the actual colour we see is determined by the proportion of the different receptors stimulated in the eye at any one time. The three basic colours are known as the **primary colours**. In scientific terminology these are red, green and blue. In the art world, yellow is sometimes considered to be one of the primary colours and this is sometimes substituted for green. Try to remember this, because seeing red, yellow and blue listed as the primary colours in a book on art can be a little confusing.

If we mix the primary colours we can obtain a new set of colours which are known as secondary or **complementary colours**. Thus, a mixture of red and green light will produce yellow; green and blue will produce cyan; and blue and red will produce magenta. These are basic colour mixes and if different amounts of coloured lights are mixed, then a range of colours will be produced.

Production of colours by this process of mixing coloured lights is known as the **additive** colour process. It forms the basis of colour television and some colour films. In colour television, the picture is built up by means of a series of tiny areas on the screen which glow in the three primary colours.

Without going into the technicalities, the colour of the television picture is built up by the number and brightness of the colours that appear in the small areas known as phosphors. A bright white screen is produced when all the colour areas are lit up; red colour appears when only the red phosphors are active; and so on. It is instructive to have a look at your television screen with a reasonably powerful magnifying glass with the brightness turned down a little and you will see the structure of the colour elements.

## The colour triangle

One method that artists use to visualise colour and colour combinations is the colour wheel. If you imagine the visible spectrum bent round to form a circle so that red joins up with violet we can produce a circle with all the colours of the spectrum blending into one another. The more we spread out the colours and the colour mixtures, the more complicated the wheel becomes. There is, however, a much simpler and more basic means of understanding colour. This is called the **colour triangle** and is a simplification of the colour wheel.

The colour triangle can be seen in Figure 11.2. On the uppermost angle we have red, on the right-hand angle we have green and on the left-hand angle, blue. We can now write in on the sides of the triangle the complementary colours which are made up of a mixture of the primaries. Thus, on the side red–green we can write yellow; on the side blue–green we write cyan; and on the side red–blue we write magenta. We now have a working diagram that will help us to understand what happens when we mix colours and when we

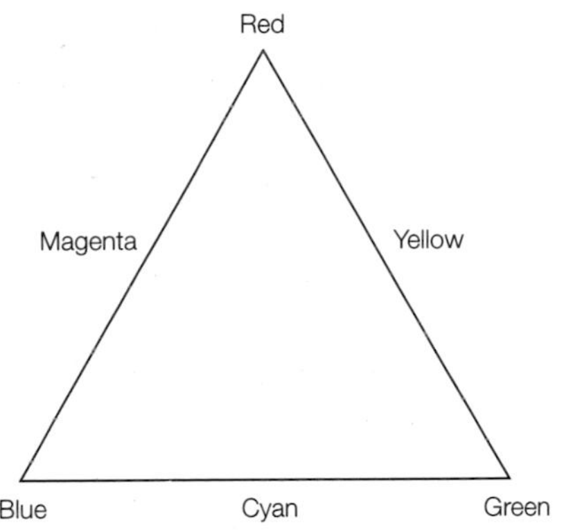


Fig. 11.2 The primary and complementary colours.

take colours away. This gives us a key to understanding how filters work, what filter to use in any situation and how colour film works. In the colour triangle remember that colours opposite one another will tend to reduce or even cancel each other.

> The triangle gives us an immediate way of working out which filter to use to get a specific effect, and also shows us how the subtractive colour process works.
>
> If you look through a coloured filter, say a red filter, everything appears red. This means that the red filter is letting through red light and cutting out light of other colours. The triangle immediately tells us what actually happens. Thus red, as we have seen, blocks blue and green. Blue will block red and green and green will block red and blue. Conversely, the complementary colours indicated on the sides of the triangle will block colours immediately opposite them. Yellow, therefore, will cut out some of the blues. We are talking about ideal cases of course. Actual filters do let through some light of other colours but they will reduce the other colours if they don't actually block them completely. In the last example a blue filter will block red and green – that is, yellow.

## The subtractive colour process

As we have seen, the additive colour process adds light of the primary colours to produce the other colours and, together, to produce white light. In the subtractive process, we remove the primary colours from white light and still produce any colour we

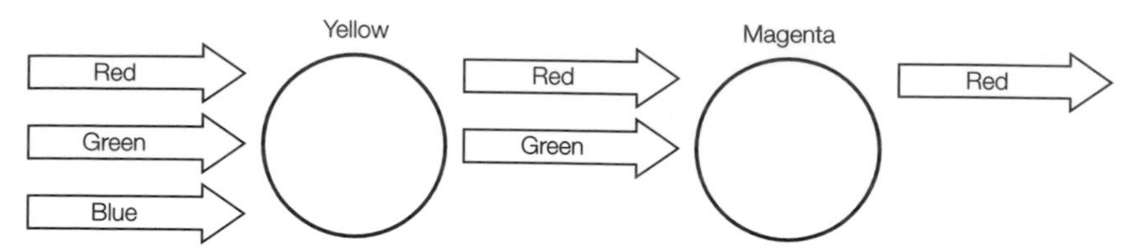


Fig. 11.3 How two filters of complementary colours can produce a primary colour from white light.

wish. This is done by using filters. The complementary colours – yellow, cyan and magenta – will absorb primaries opposite them on the colour triangle so these are used in the subtractive colour process. Figure 11.3 shows how this is done.

## Object colour

When light reaches the surface of an object, three things can happen: the light can be absorbed; or it can be transmitted through the object; or it can be reflected by the object. Any of these reactions can occur, or any combination of them. If an object appears black, it means that no light has been reflected back to the eye. If an object is red, it means it has absorbed blue and green light and reflected back just red light. An object that is yellow has reflected red and green and has absorbed blue. A white object has reflected all the light falling on it.

### Colour descriptions

A **hue** is a name given to the principal colours on the colour wheel. **Value** is an expression used to describe a colour's darkness or lightness. **Tints** describe the amount of white added to a pure colour and **shades** is the opposite situation when black is added to a pure colour. Sometimes the word **tone** is used to describe colours which are no longer pure hues. **Saturation** describes the purity of a hue.

### Colour composition

Colour composition is a complex subject. Much has been written on the subject of colour harmony and even Kodak suggests that 'colour harmony is complex and very largely a matter of personal taste'.

In very general terms, colours which lie close to one another in the spectrum, or colour wheel, tend to be harmonious and look pleasant when used together. Colours opposite each other on the colour wheel, or colour triangle, give strong colour contrasts. We shall discuss colour composition in more detail below.

**Colour heat** Red, orange, brown and yellow are often regarded as being 'warm' colours. On the other hand, blues and greens are the so-called 'cool' colours. When reds and oranges predominate in a picture, a 'warmer' effect will be given than when blues and greens predominate.

**Colour movement** To our eyes, the warm colours appear to be nearer than the cold colours. Whereas red and orange in a picture look close up, blues appear to be further away. Green is a neutral colour. Using these facts, an impression of distance can be given in a photograph by ensuring that there are warm colours in the foreground and cooler colours in the background. If we think for a moment why this should be, bear in mind that, in nature, the warm colours such as reds and yellows are often the colours of flowers that we observe near to us and to which we are attracted. The grass, green vegetation and blue sky are naturally in the background, so we perceive them as receding.

**Lighting** Lighting has a very big effect indeed on colours. The colour of objects is greatly influenced by the intensity of light, its direction and the colour quality of the light itself. We shall consider this later, but first we must discuss how colour film works.

## Colour film

At present, two types of colour film are readily available: those that use the subtractive colour process and those that use the additive colour process. Most films use the subtractive process. The only film that uses the additive process is Polachrome 35-mm slide film.

Subtractive colour film is available as slide film which produces transparencies or negative film from which prints are made. You can always tell whether a film is designed for transparencies or prints because transparency films end in the word 'chrome' whereas colour negative films, producing prints, end in the word 'color' or 'colour'. Thus Koda*chrome* and Fuji*chrome* produce colour slides; Koda*color* and Fuji*color* produce colour negatives which need to be printed.

Colour films, both for the production of slides and colour negatives, are available in a similar range of speeds to black and white films. Slow films are available at ISO 25/15 to 50/18. There are medium-speed films around 100/21 and faster films range from 200/24 to 1000/31 and even higher.

The characteristics of colour film, because the initial image is a silver one, closely follow the characteristics of black and white film. The faster the film, the grainier it is and the lower the definition. Films up to ISO 125/22 give very good results and the grain is fine. Colour rendition, too, is very good. ISO 200/24 films are beginning to look grainy and the colours tend to be warmer and less saturated. In excess of ISO 400/27, films look very grainy and the colours less saturated.

The best results are always obtained with slower films. Nevertheless, astonishing results have been obtained with the faster ones. As a general rule, these fast films should only be used when light levels are low and there is a need to capture fast action.

Recently some manufacturers have brought out substantially improved colour negative material. The Kodak Ektar range is one example. Unless you require big, very high quality enlargements, such films will not give you noticeably better results than standard colour negative materials. They can be also somewhat temperamental in use.

## Colour from black and white

All readily available colour films have one thing in common. Their first stage is always the production of a black and white negative image using the formation of metallic silver from silver halides. During processing the metallic silver disappears and is replaced by coloured dyes which act as colour filters.

## Reversal colour film

During the processing of colour slide films a process called 'reversal' occurs. In this process the negative is changed to a positive.

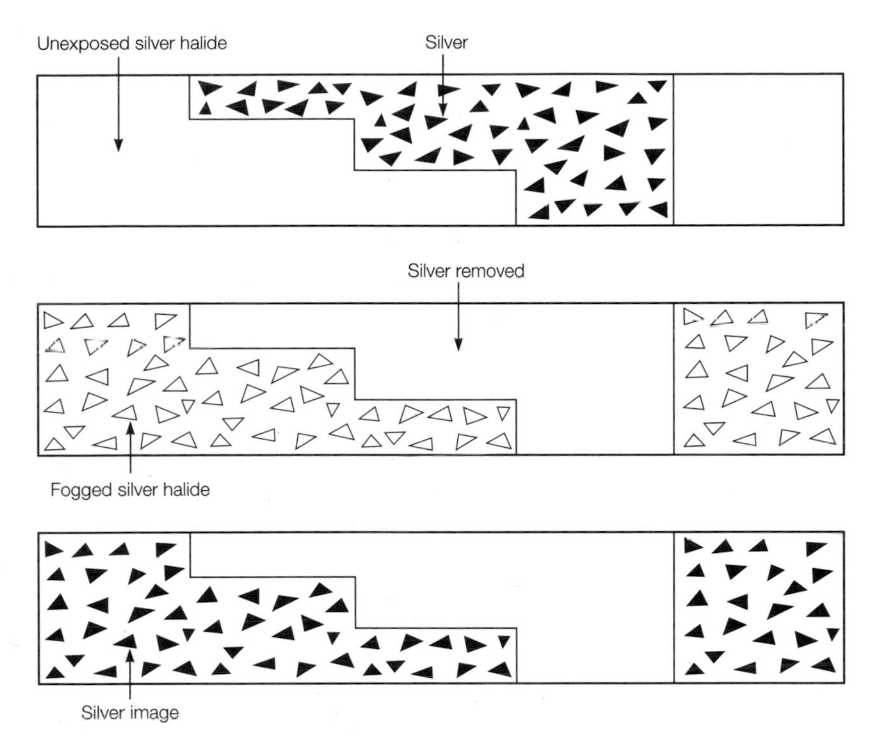


Fig. 11.4 The reversal process in black and white film.

## The process of reversal

When a black and white film is exposed and then developed – but not fixed – we have the situation where there is present a negative image made up of metallic silver grains that have been developed. There is also present in the emulsion the silver halide crystals that were not affected by light and so were not developed. The bright highlight areas will contain more silver grains and very little silver halide. In the shadow areas very little silver will be present but most of the original silver halide will remain. If we were to remove the metallic silver and develop the remaining silver halide, converting it in its turn to silver, we would produce a reversed image. Because the shadow areas contain a good deal of silver halide, these will become the darkest areas of the image. The bright areas, containing little silver halide, will end up as bright clear areas on the film. We thus produce a positive image in black and white. This is known as the reversal process and is shown diagrammatically in Figure 11.4.

The reversal process can, of course, be used to produce black and white positive slides. One manufacturer, Agfa, produces a reversal film. This film is designed specifically for black and white slides. However, by suitable processing, it is possible to produce black and white positive slides from black and white negative films. Best results are obtained with the slower films and at least one manufacturer, Tetenal, produces reversal processing kits. Ilford XP2 processed in E6 (reversal) chemistry will also produce positive monochrome transparencies.

## The production of colour

In the subtractive colour process producing positive slides, the original picture is produced as a black and white image using silver halide. During the reversal process dyes are produced. The silver is then removed. A dye image is left and this uses the principle of subtraction of colours from white light to produce the final colour image.

Colour film has three separate black and white emulsions. These are placed one on top of the other. The top layer is blue sensitive, the middle layer is green sensitive and the bottom layer is red sensitive. The structure of a basic colour reversal film is shown in Figure 11.5.

A complication exists in that the green-sensitive and red-sensitive emulsions are also sensitive to blue light. Some means are necessary, therefore, to prevent or diminish the amount of blue light reaching

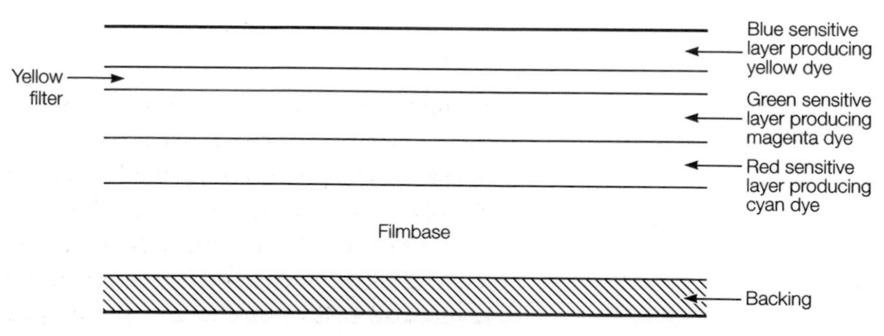


Fig. 11.5 Structure of a colour slide film.

the green- and red-sensitive layers. This is done by inserting a thin yellow filter between the blue- and green-sensitive layers, as shown in Figure 11.5. When the picture is taken, each emulsion layer produces its own black and white image in proportion to the amounts of blue, green and red in the original subject. These images can be imagined as being one on top of the other.

During the reversal process, colour development takes place. In the emulsion, colour couplers are present and dyes are produced. The amount of dye is in exact proportion to the amount of silver present in the positive image. The amount of dye produced is, therefore, in proportion to the amounts of blue, green and red in the subject.

The colours of the dyes produced in three layers are complementary to the colour sensitivity of each layer: the blue-sensitive layer produces yellow dye; the green-sensitive layer produces magenta dye; the red-sensitive area produces cyan dye. At this stage of reversal colour film processing, we have on the film three black and white positive images, three black and white negative images and three dye images, all superimposed.

The next stage is to remove all the silver by the bleaching process. When we view the washed and dried film, the dye layers act as filters when light passes through the transparency and removes colours from white light and so produces the original colours of the subject. Figure 11.6 shows how this is done.

## Review

**Follow any colour through to see how it is reproduced on the film. If we take green as an example, see how in the negative image silver grains are formed in the green-sensitive layer and in the blue-sensitive and red-sensitive layers, silver halide remains. During reversal and colour development, silver halide is converted to black metallic silver in the blue- and red-sensitive layers and yellow and cyan dyes are produced. The silver is removed and we are left with yellow and cyan dyes. On**

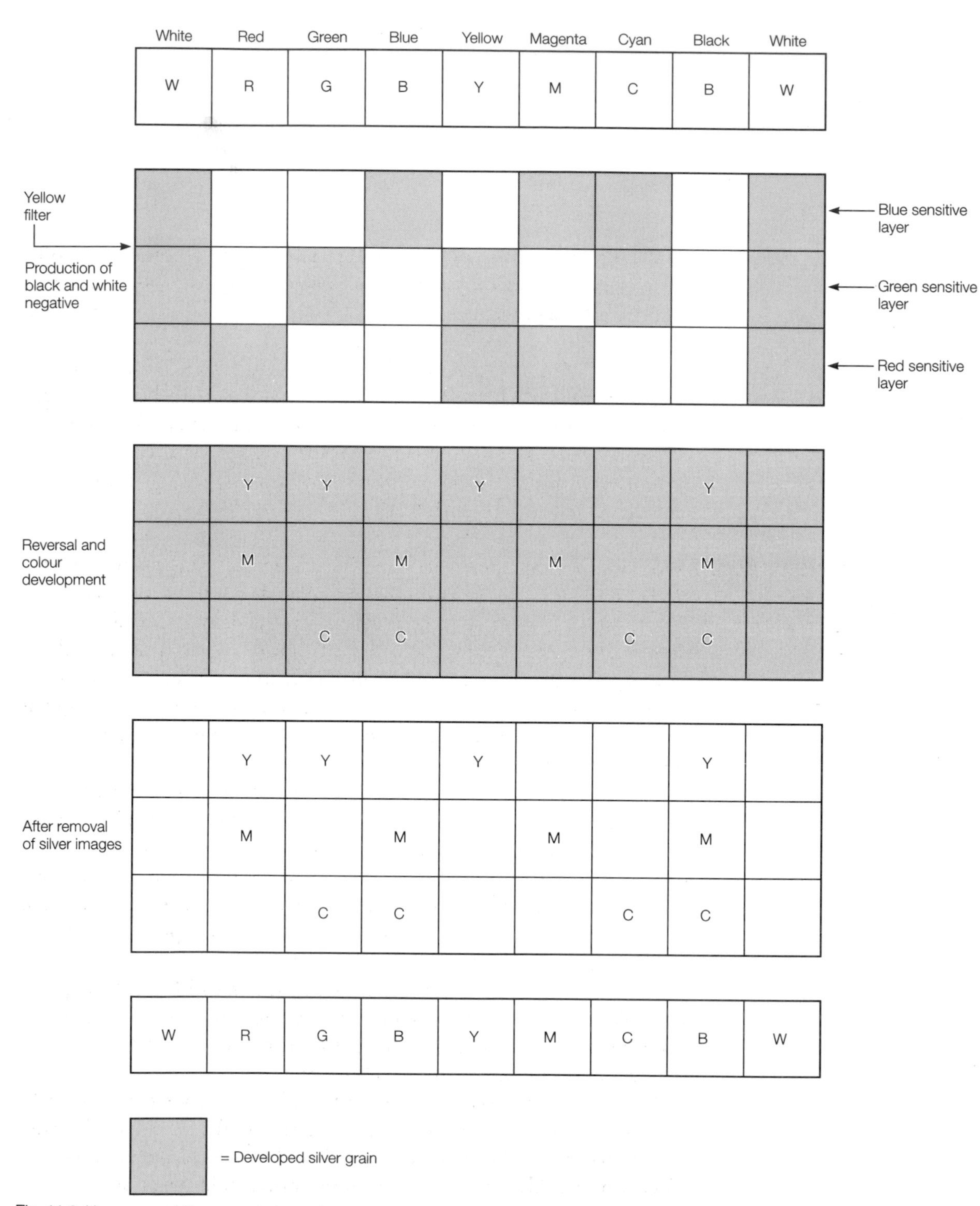


Fig. 11.6 How reversal film reproduces colour.

**projection, yellow and cyan will remove blue and red from white light and will allow green light to pass through so that area of the slide will be green.**

This is the principle of all subtractive colour slide films. There are variations in detail between individual films. Some have more layers than others and, in the case of Kodachrome, processing is more complex and can only be done in specially equipped laboratories. Most slide films are easier to process and processing kits for home processing are readily available.

## The additive colour film process

If we photograph a scene using red, blue or green filters, the filters allow the light of their own colour to pass and affect the silver emulsion of the film. Other colours are blocked or reduced.

In additive colour films, the photograph is taken through a colour mosaic which is printed on the film. This mosaic is composed of very many tiny red, blue and green filters. If we photograph a green object, the silver halide behind the green filters will be affected and will develop into silver grains.

When the reversal process is carried out those grains will be removed and there will be a clear area behind the green areas of the mosaic. When white light is passed through the film, those areas, originally green in the subject, will allow green light to pass. In the red and blue areas the silver grains will have been formed during the reversal process. On viewing, the silver grains will prevent light passing through the red and green filters.

Previously available colour processes used the additive principle. Notable among these were Autochrome and Dufaycolor. Today only Polachrome 35-mm instant colour film uses the additive process and, of course, colour television.

There are some disadvantages to the additive process. Films tend to be slow and the resulting transparencies are dense. This is because the photograph is both taken through and projected through the filter mosaic. Also the mosaic becomes noticeable when big enlargements are made.

## Colour negative film

The subtractive colour process is also used for the production of colour negatives. Colour negatives can be printed to produce positive colour prints. Fundamentally the production of colour prints is very similar to the production of colour slides. The main difference is that the process occurs in two stages.

Colour negative film is essentially the same as slide film. Basically it consists of the blue-, green- and red-sensitive layers. In processing colour negative film, the basic difference between that and the processing of slide film is that reversal does not take place, and during the development of the silver negatives colour development also takes place. When the negative silver image is removed, the colour negative remains with all the original colours appearing as their complementary colours.

Colour printing paper also has three colour-sensitive emulsions which, during the development process, produce dye images in exactly the same way as both colour negative film and slide film. When the print is made from a colour negative, the light and dark tones are reversed and the colours also are reversed. A positive print showing the tones and colours of the original scene is the result.

When a colour print is viewed in white light, part of the spectrum is absorbed by the dyes in the emulsion in just the same way as dyes in the slide absorb transmitted light. The picture reflected back from the white paper surface then appears to us in full colour. Although it is easily possible to illuminate a colour print so that it has the same overall brightness as the image produced on the screen by a projected slide, the image quality of the latter is invariably superior. It is likely to have higher colour saturation than a print and it will have higher contrast in the all-important lightest and darkest tones.

If we want to make colour prints from slides, this can be done by making an intermediate negative and then a print from that negative. Alternatively, direct reversal paper exists which works in the same way as a colour slide and this can be used to produce a colour print directly from the positive slide. These papers do not rely on colour development but have colorants already incorporated in their three emulsions. These tend to have better colour characteristics than the best dyes obtained by chromogenic development and their light fastness is superior. Nevertheless a colour print always has a much more restricted luminance range than a slide. Whereas a print has a maximum luminance range of about 100 to 1, a slide can show a range in excess of 1000 to 1.

Primary colours, complementary colours and the order of colour-sensitive emulsions of a colour film are often difficult to remember. There is, however, a simple way to remember them which involves the colour triangle and a key word. The rest can be worked out provided, of course, that you remember the key word. The word is BEGGAR. The consonants in this word give you the initial letters of the three primary colours: B for blue, G for green and R for red. These colours, as we know, are placed on the apexes of the triangle. On the sides of the triangle are the mixtures. These are red–blue (magenta), blue–green (cyan), green–red (yellow). Even if you forget the names of the complementary colours, it would be sufficient for examination purposes, to describe them as mixtures of the colours. We have already seen how the triangle gives a key to which colours block which.

Finally, the order of the colours in our word (beggar) gives the order of sensitivity of the emulsions on subtractive colour film. Namely *blue* sensitive, *green* sensitive and *red* sensitive. The only additional thing one needs to remember is the yellow filter between the blue- and green-sensitive emulsion layers.

## Colour film exposure

Exposure latitude for colour films is much less that it is for black and white. Therefore, getting exposure as near correct as possible is more important when shooting in colour. As latitude for colour slide film may be as little as one stop, correct exposure is vital. Because latitude is low, colour films will not tolerate as much contrast in the scene as black and white. It is important, therefore, to control contrast as much as possible.

The effect of incorrect exposure is different in the case of slide film and negative film. Slight over-exposure with colour transparencies leads to desaturated colours and the slide looks wishy-washy. Moderate under-exposure is much more acceptable to the eye. Although rather dense slides are produced, the colours tend to be more saturated. In the case of colour negatives, slight over-exposure is preferable and more satisfactory prints will be obtained. Even moderate under-exposure, as far as colour negatives are concerned, leads to poor colour and contrast in the resulting print.

Because the latitude for both over- and under-exposure is limited in colour film, it is useful to bracket your exposures. A good guideline is to take a minimum of three pictures: one at the indicated exposure, one at a half stop more, and another a half stop less. In addition, reflectors and fill-in flash to add light in shadow areas can improve colour pictures.

## Colour temperature

Our eyes adapt very quickly to the colour quality of light. We accept as white light quite a wide range of colours of light which are in fact anything but pure white. Thus noon daylight seems white to us and the household electric lighting in the evening appears just as white.

Actually artificial light is very much redder than daylight. We can see this is so at twilight if we look into a room from outside when the electric light in the room has been switched on. The light inside the room, when viewed from outside, looks very red indeed. As soon as we enter the room, however, our eyes adapt and we accept the light as being white.

Colour film cannot adapt to the colour temperature of light. During manufacture, the colour response of the three emulsions has to be balanced for the kind of light in which it is going to be used to take photographs. Daylight film is balanced for the colour temperature of average midday sunlight plus some skylight. It gives its most satisfactory results, therefore, when exposed in light of this colour temperature. Artificial light colour films are balanced for the much more reddish colour temperature of studio lighting.

The actual colour quality of light is termed *colour temperature*. The unit of measurement is the kelvin (K). One kelvin is the same as one degree Celsius. The kelvin scale is similar to the absolute scale of temperatures. We refer to colour 'temperature' because the degree figures refer to the temperature to which you would need to heat a standard laboratory object, known as a perfect black body, for it to admit light of the colour quality in which you are interested. We all are familiar with the red glow of the elements of an electric toaster when it is switched on. You would need to heat a 'perfect black body' to a temperature of 5500 K for it to emit light equivalent to average midday sunlight or electronic flash. It is this colour temperature that daylight colour films are balanced for: 3400 K is the colour temperature of most photoflood lamps; 3200 K is the temperature of tungsten studio lamps; 2700 K to 2900 K is the colour temperature of ordinary household lamps; and a candle has a colour temperature of 1900 K.

## Filters

When using slide film, it is important to make sure that the film you use is balanced for the kind of lighting you use. If you use daylight film to take a picture in tungsten lighting, then your picture will be much too red. A correction can be made by using a colour conversion filter over your lens. Such filters, often known as 'D–A', are bluish in colour. 'A–D' filters, which are brownish-red, can be used when artificial light-balanced film is exposed to daylight. If you did not use a filter, then the picture would have a very blue appearance when artificial light-balanced film is exposed in daylight.

Electronic flash tends to have colour temperatures about the same as noon sunlight or perhaps a little bluer. Sometimes a slightly warming filter such as Kodak 81A might be useful when exposing daylight film with some makes of electronic flash.

In the case of colour negative film that is designed for exposing in daylight, corrections are possible during the printing process but such corrections are sometimes not made by the photo-finisher especially if only one or two artificial light shots are included in the same film as a majority of daylight exposures. It is not really necessary, therefore, to use conversion or light-balancing filters on the camera lens when working in artificial light. However, using a colour correction filter can avoid later problems with your processor.

In general terms, outdoor scenes at night, where there is artificial light, produce more natural looking results using artificial light-balanced film. However, daylight colour films work satisfactorily if the very reddish look of artificial light is acceptable.

Fluorescent lighting is very difficult to photograph in colour, because the light emitted by fluorescent tubes invariably has peaks in one or more regions of the spectrum, their locations depending on the particular type of tube. It is difficult to correct for such peaks by using filters. Tubes known as 'cool white', which are very widely used, have a pronounced peak in the green region, and a 30 magenta colour compensation filter on the camera lens provides quite effective correction for cool white fluorescent illumination. There is an FLD filter that corrects for cool white fluorescent illumination when using daylight slide film and an FLT filter for tungsten-balanced film. Because fluorescent lighting is so varied, preliminary tests are advisable before exposing a lot of film.

## Mixed light sources

If you mix light sources of different colour temperatures it is not a practical proposition to correct for them all. Thus, electronic flash should not be used when the main light is, for example, a photoflood lamp. Unusual, sometimes 'creative', results can be obtained, but individual experiment is the only way to discover what is going to happen.

## Exposure and colour correction filters

Colour correction filters – certainly those converting colour temperature from daylight to artificial or artificial to daylight – are fairly dense and so filter factors can be quite high. For instance, D–A filters need a two-stop increase. An ISO 100/21 film, therefore, would be reduced to ISO 32/16. A–D filters need slightly under one stop more exposure, which would reduce an ISO 160/23 film to about ISO 100/21.

## UV–skylight filters

These filters are often useful for removing excess blue from scenes where there is an excess of ultraviolet light, such as mountain views. They will also help to remove an excess of blue in snow and beach scenes. Such filters have little or no effect on normal scenes and can remain on the end of a lens where they not only remove excess blue but also protect the front element.

## Colour composition

In Chapter 1 we discussed aspects of good composition in a photograph. Although we were discussing black and white photography, the same considerations apply when taking pictures in colour. The same three fundamental guidelines should be adhered to. These guidelines are that your photograph needs to have a theme, you need to draw attention to or emphasise your subject and, above all, you need to keep the photograph as simple as possible. Colour is just another compositional tool you can use.

Colour can be used to set the mood of your photograph. A picture which contains mainly greens and blues tends to be quiet and tranquil. A picture with vibrant reds and yellows, on the other hand, conveys much more lively feelings.

You can use saturated contrasting colours to draw attention to your subject. A line of red-painted beach huts can be very striking indeed against the blues of the sea and sky and the yellow of the sand. As we have said, the cooler colours, blues and greens, appear to recede and the reds, oranges and yellows appear to advance; therefore, blues and greens are very good background colours. A bright red background for a portrait would not work very well unless a special effect was desired, because the red background would tend to overpower the subject.

However, as in other areas of composition, rules are made to be broken. The ultimate test of a good colour composition is the *use* of colour, and all the other elements that go towards good composition stand or fall by the ultimate test of whether the picture pleases you and whether it gets over the appropriate message that you wished it to give to the viewer. This is just as true for colour photography as it is for black and white.

### Viewing colour pictures

The effect of colour pictures will change depending on the illumination in which they are viewed. As far as slides are concerned, projection is the best way to view them. You need a reasonable quality projector and, most important, a reasonable quality screen.

Slides projected on a wall will not look their best, particularly if the wall has an off-white colour. Viewers are quite useful, specially those using a back projection technique onto a screen. A light table, which is a white translucent piece of glass or plastic lit from below, is an excellent way of viewing and sorting slides. Slides viewed by holding them up to the light or at the window often look bluer than they should.

Colour prints can be viewed either in artificial light or daylight but, as with slides, they sometimes look bluer than they should when viewed in daylight.

### Further Reading

*Basic Photography* and *Advanced Photography*, both by Michael Langford and published by Focal Press.
Also really excellent, but sadly out of print, is: *Color as Seen and Photographed*, published by Eastman Kodak, USA. If you can pick up one second hand don't fail to do so.

## Summary

**In this chapter we have described how we see colour, discussed colour temperature and described how colour films work, both by additive and subtractive synthesis. Taking colour into consideration when composing pictures has also been discussed.**

# 12 Portraiture

The aim of this chapter is to cover the basic principles of portrait photography. When you have completed this chapter you will be able to set up basic lighting, the kind used in studio portraiture, conduct a studio portrait session, use the most suitable lighting and poses for your subject and be able to minimise facial defects and unattractive features. You will be able to apply your knowledge of studio portraiture to location and outdoor portraiture.

Portraiture, in the context of this book, is the photography of people and animals in such a way as to portray character. Portraits include close-ups of faces, head and shoulder pictures, three-quarter length views, pictures containing two or more subjects and groups of subjects.

While a portrait is essentially a photograph of an individual or individuals, it should be more than that. It should convey to the viewer something of the personality of the sitter and, in location portraiture, the interests and possibly occupation of the subject.

Portraits can be taken in a studio, they can be taken outdoors or they can be location portraits showing people in their homes or work environment. Portraits can be of one or more people or of people with their pets. Effective portraits can be taken of domestic and wild animals.

We shall start by looking at some fundamental aspects of portraiture, first of all in the studio. It does not matter if you have no studio facilities of your own. It is very easy to set up your own simple studio at home. You can start initially with a plain background and with one light. The light can be a small portable electronic flash unit with an extension lead so that it can be used off the camera. Supplementary lighting can be a simple reflector. The guidelines we shall discuss work just as well with simple equipment as they do with more complicated lighting, whether it is studio electronic flash or tungsten lights.

First of all find a suitable location in your home where you can set up a temporary studio. If at all possible you will need room to place your subject between 4 and 6 ft in front of a plain background and to place your lighting on either side of the subject. You will also need to put your camera between 8 and 10 ft in front of the subject.

## Perspective in portraiture

Before we think about setting up lighting, let us first consider perspective in relation to photographing a person's face. Perspective distortion occurs if the camera you are using is too near the subject. Parts of the picture near the camera become too large compared with more distant objects in the picture. As mentioned earlier, we are all familiar with amusing pictures showing very large feet in the foreground and a very small face in the distance. This change in size relationship occurs with the human face too, so that a nose can look much bigger than it actually is.

Wide-angle lenses can be particularly troublesome and make noses, foreheads and chins far too large. Even the so-called normal lens with a focal length of 50 mm for 35-mm cameras is really too short where the subject's head and shoulders only fill the frame. Lenses with longer focal lengths, like 90 mm with 35-mm cameras, will give more pleasant and natural looking results. Focal lengths between 75 and 135 mm all work well for portrait work with 35-mm cameras.

Above 135 mm focal length, the opposite effect occurs – compression of planes – and faces begin to look flat. With longer focal length lenses it is necessary to be quite some distance from the subject, making it difficult to use a normal sized room as a studio.

However, we can still take satisfactory portraits using a normal lens or even moderately wide-angle lenses if we take care not to get too near the subject but take three-quarter-length shots. Later the negative can be enlarged just to include the head and shoulders if that is what is required. Also, by taking a little extra care in posing the model, the more noticeable manifestations of perspective distortion can be eliminated. Instead of the model looking straight at the camera (which should seldom occur in any case), he or she can turn slightly in one direction or the other so that the nose will not appear too prominent in the picture.

## Review

**Ideally a lens of around 90 mm in focal length with a 35-mm camera will work very well indeed, or if you have a zoom lens, then set it at around 90 to 100 mm.**

## Camera viewpoint

As a general rule the camera lens should be level with the subject's face, and slightly higher than the tip of the subject's nose. It is generally not considered good practice to 'look up your model's nostrils'.

The general rules for determining exposures are the same for portrait photography as they are for most other branches of photography. However, there are one or two things you need to look out for. If you are using studio electronic flash and have a flash meter, the problem is much simpler. Most flash meters measure incident light. If you are using tungsten lighting, the incident light method of exposure measurement nearly always requires a separate meter. The Weston Euromaster or the Sekonic Studio L-398 exposure meters work well. If, however, you must rely on metering through the lens of your camera or on a reflected light meter reading, then be careful that light from the background or stray light from a lamp does not give you an incorrect reading. If possible, take a substitute reading from the position of the model. A Kodak 18 per cent grey card is excellent for this purpose. Alternatively, you can take a meter reading directly off your subject's face, making corrections as described in Chapter 5. If you have any doubts about exposure, use the bracketing technique.

From the point of view of exposure determination the main light is of primary importance. The fill-in light or other effect lights do not normally contribute much to the overall level of light. However, a final check of the exposure with all lights on is a good idea. (See Chapter 7.)

The best result will usually show only one set of shadows in your portrait and, as a general rule, the most satisfactory pictures can be obtained if the light casting those shadows is high and to one side of the camera – in other words, as if it were the sun.

Other positions of the lights are quite possible, however. Faces lit from below have a bizarre and somewhat frightening appearance. When you have mastered simple basic lighting, you should

We are all accustomed to seeing objects lit by one light source – namely, the sun. This, of course, casts one set of shadows. We prefer, therefore, to see objects lit by one light source only and generally find more than one set of shadows in the picture very disturbing as these can spoil an otherwise good photograph. This is a good basic rule for all photography but it is particularly applicable in portrait work.

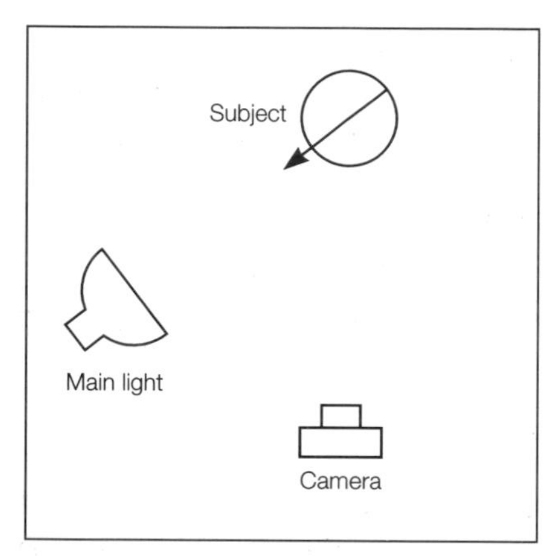

Fig. 12.1

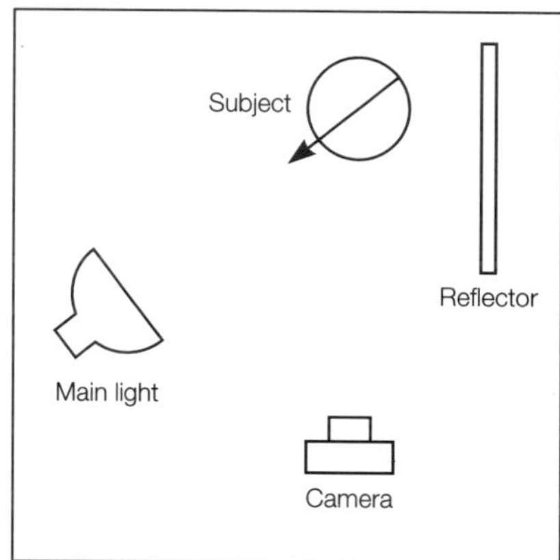

Fig. 12.2

experiment with different light positions, but you will probably find the most attractive studio portraits will be obtained by imitating the sun and having your main light high up and to one side of the camera. This often produces flattering results and is therefore more likely to please your sitter.

## Review

**Unless you are aiming for a very specific effect that you have in mind, then a good working guide as to whether or not you have produced a good portrait is to ask your sitter whether he or she likes it. If the model likes your picture, it is probably a good portrait.**

The main light, sometimes known as the key light, is the most important in a studio set-up. It not only determines the position of the shadows on your model's face but it also sets the mood of the picture and influences the general appearance of your model's face. Figure 12.1 shows a typical position for the main light, which could be a floodlamp or an electronic flash unit.

The light is positioned higher than the subject's head and about 45 degrees to one side of the camera–subject line. The main light is usually between 3½ and 4½ ft away from your subject's head.

When you have set up a main light as shown in Figure 12.1, check the shadow areas it produces. Make sure that the light is above the level of your subject's head and move it around noting how the position of the shadows change, particularly the shadow falling from the subject's nose. With tungsten lighting this is a very easy exercise; but not so easy if you are using electronic flash.

---

## Exercise

Try a few photographs as you move the position of the light and do make careful records of just where the lights are for each photograph you take so that you can refer later to your notes when the pictures are printed.

---

The use of only one light produces very heavy shadows and the result will be contrasty. To reduce the contrast we can use a reflector in roughly the position shown in Figure 12.2. This reflects some of the light from your key light back into the shadow.

---

## Exercise

Move the reflector about, watching for the maximum amount of reflected light falling into the shadows. Your reflector can be a sheet of white cardboard or you can make one from crumpled aluminium foil pasted to a piece of cardboard. Also very effective is a piece of shiny plastic survival blanket pasted on a piece of cardboard. These survival blankets are usually obtainable from your local sports shop and are unexpensive.

---

A more easily controllable way of reducing contrast is to use a fill-in light. In Figure 12.3 we show where a fill-in light can be positioned.

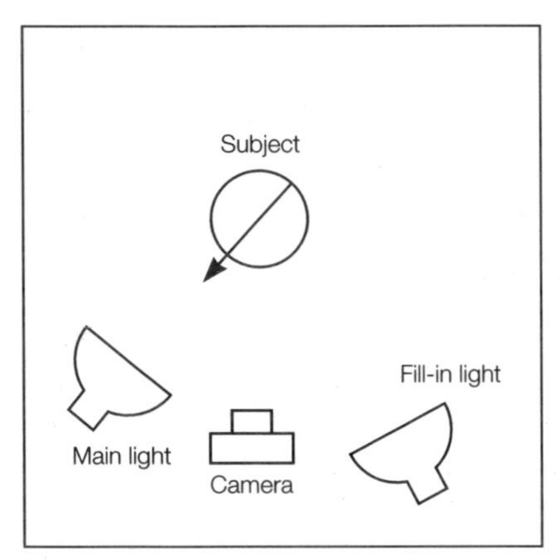


Fig. 12.3

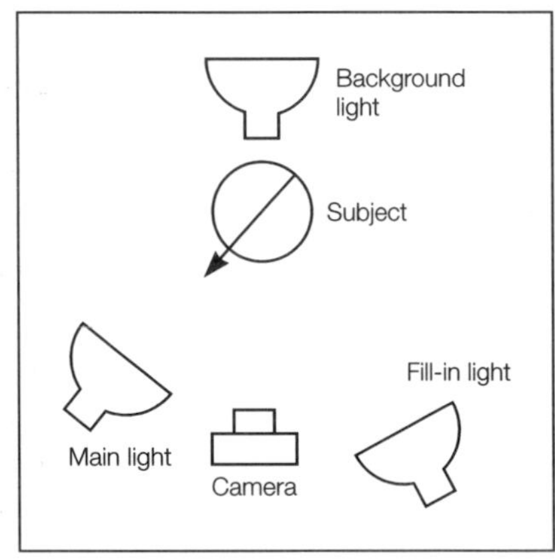


Fig. 12.4

The fill-in light should be a much more diffused light than the main or key light and should be placed roughly at the position of the camera. For black and white photography, it is a good idea to have the fill-in light at roughly one or two stops less in intensity than the key light. In colour photography only one or possibly even a half stop difference will give satisfactory results. The intensity of lights can be decreased by moving them further from the subject, or increased by moving them nearer the subject. Remember, of course, that the inverse square law is just as applicable in studio lighting as elsewhere (see Chapter 7). Any diffused shadow cast by the fill-in light should fall out of the camera's view, possibly shielded by the subject.

## Review

**When setting up your lights, always work to the plan detailed below. Position your key light, paying special attention to the shadows. Measure the exposure required by the key light. Turn the key light off. Position the fill-in light, taking care that it does not produce its own obvious shadows. Move the fill-in light backwards and forwards until it gives an exposure reading which**

**is the required number of stops less than the key light. Turn both lights on, measure exposure, then take your picture.**

---

## Exercise

You should take a series of pictures using the lighting arrangement in Figure 12.3 then assess the pictures carefully and look for any evidence of double shadows. Work out which of your lights has produced the unwanted shadows and next time you set up the lights take special care that the offending light does not cause the same problem again.

---

Additional lighting can be used as well as your main and fill-in lights. These can include a background light and accent lights.

A **background light** is light independent of both main and fill-in lights and is used to change the tone of the background or, perhaps, to eliminate shadows cast by the key light on the background (see Figure 12.4). Remember that in a simple two-light set-up, the background will *always* be darker than your subject simply because your subject is nearer the lights. When setting up background lighting, take care that none of it spills onto your subject. Background lighting can be used to make your subject stand out from the background, to provide a circle of light behind your subject or even to project attractive patterns in the background. Pure white backgrounds can be produced by lighting the background with about four stops brighter light than that falling on the subject. If the background is lit at about the same intensity as the subject, a problem can occur in black and white photography in that skin tones can merge with the background. This does not usually occur, however, in colour portraiture unless the background is the same colour as the subject's skin.

**Accent lights** can be used effectively to illuminate particular areas of your subject (Figure 12.5). Thus, a spotlight could be used

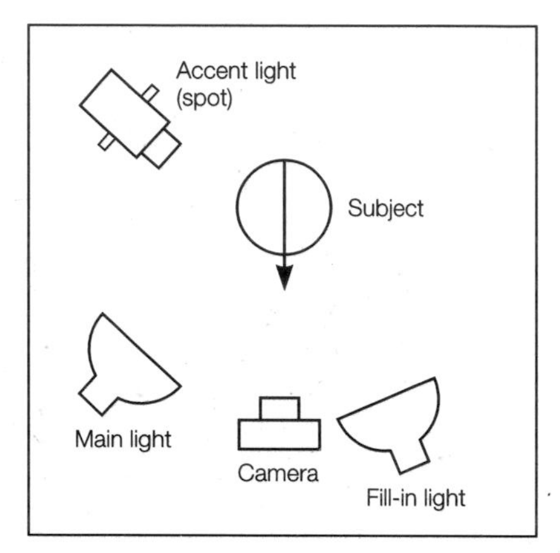


Fig. 12.5

to add highlights to your model's hair. Here, too, care must be taken when positioning the lights to make sure that no light spills onto other parts of your subject.

Lighting the hair is vital if you take a portrait of a dark-haired model against a dark background. Otherwise hair can vanish into the background.

## Review

**It is easy to avoid lighting problems if you follow two simple rules:**

- **Switch on one light at a time and observe the shadows.**
- **Switch that light off before switching on another light.**

**So, if you were arranging a four light set-up, you would adjust your key-light first with no other lights on. When you are pleased with the effect, switch off the main light. Switch on and position the fill-in light next. Turn off the fill-in light and try the background light, watching the effect as with all lights from the camera position. Finally, try the accent light by itself. When you**

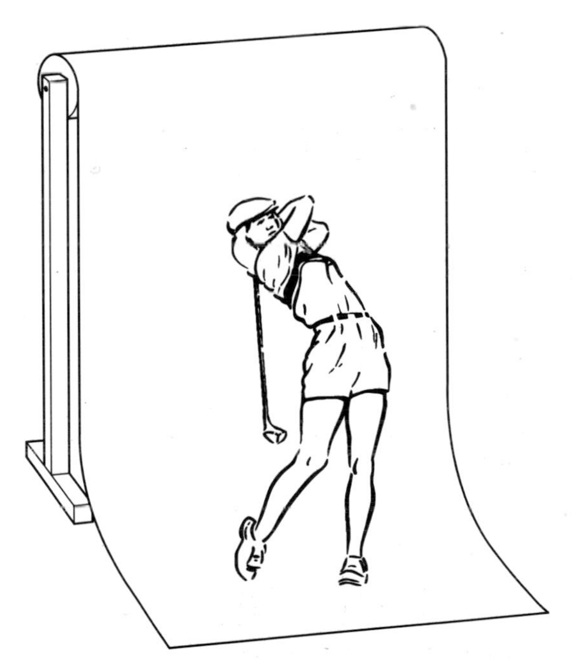

Fig. 12.6 Model posing against background paper roll.

**are quite satisfied with all these effects then turn on all the lights, make a final measurement of the exposure and start taking your pictures.**

**When lighting backgrounds remember that the tone of the background will depend on the intensity of the light falling on it. If there is no background light, then the background will always be darker in tone than the subject. If the intensity of the background light is greater than that of the main light, then the background will appear white or very much lighter in tone than the subject.**

In studio portraiture, backgrounds should be kept simple. Plain backgrounds are good. Grey or white or mottled backgrounds, which can include lightly painted cloud effects, are also very suitable. Figure 12.6 shows how background paper can be used to achieve a plain, seamless background for a full-length shot.

In colour portraiture, cool colours like blues, particularly light blue, can be very pleasant. It is best not to use bright colours, particularly reds, oranges and yellows, as areas of these colours can easily dominate the entire photograph. A problem in colour portraiture can be that coloured light reflected off a coloured background onto the model can create an unwanted colour reflection or cast which will show up in the print. Watch out for this.

## Review

**The further your model is from the background, the less chance there is of colour casts. Also, the further your model is from the background, within reason, the easier it is to make sure that the shadow cast by the model from the main light falls out of camera view. A distance of about 5 or 6 ft is usually quite sufficient to avoid colour casts and make sure that the model's shadow falls outside the picture.**

Portrait lighting is usually classified by the way in which the shadows cast by the key light fall on the model's features. The three main types of studio lighting are:

- broad lighting
- short lighting
- paramount lighting (glamour or butterfly lighting)

Remember that a portrait of a person's face taken square-on to the camera is usually not the most satisfactory position unless there is some very good reason for it. The most attractive portraits are usually taken with the model's face turned to the right or left, but seldom more than 45 degrees to the camera–subject line. Angles much greater than 45 degrees produce profile effects.

In **broad lighting** (Figure 12.7) the subject's face is turned a little to the right or left of the camera–subject line. The key light is

Fig. 12.7 Broad lighting.

Fig. 12.8 Short lighting.

Fig. 12.9 Paramount or glamour lighting.

positioned so that it illuminates the subject's cheek nearest the camera, and the shadow cast by the model's nose falls down to the corner of the lip. There is a triangle of light on the cheek furthest from the key light.

In **short lighting** (Figure 12.8) the model's face is again turned slightly to one side. However, the key light now illuminates the model's cheek furthest from the camera. The small triangle of light now appears on the model's cheek nearest the camera and the shadows are also on that side.

Short lighting is also known as 'Rembrandt' lighting because that great painter often favoured this type of lighting for his portrait subjects.

In **paramount** or **glamour lighting** (Figure 12.9) the key light is high up and directly in front of the subject's face and the shadow of the nose appears on the upper lip, its shape looking a little like butterfly wings – hence the name 'butterfly' is sometimes used to describe this type of lighting. This lighting is also known as 'glamour' lighting because it is particularly flattering to the female face.

The effect of the three basic forms of lighting are shown in Figures 12.7, 12.8 and 12.9, and the appearance of the model can be seen to change with each type of lighting. Which lighting do you think makes the model's face appear rounder, and which makes the face look thinner?

Unless you are aiming for specific, dramatic or character study results, a good general rule is to make your subject look his or her best. In other words, aim to please your model and choose the lighting that is best for that purpose.

### Review

**Remember the following rules:**

**Broad lighting makes the face look broader and rounder and short lighting will make the face appear narrower and longer. So, if your model has a plump face, then try short lighting. Paramount or glamour lighting is a very flattering form of lighting for female models. It is often used on television for lighting young lady news readers. Next time you watch a news broadcast or female interviewers or interviewees, look for the characteristic butterfly shadow under the subject's nose. Figures 12.10 to 12.13 present further examples of the effective use of broad or short lighting.**

---

## Exercise

Now you are ready to try the effects of studio lighting for yourself. Choose a subject and take a series of photographs of that person using short lighting, broad lighting and paramount lighting. Make careful notes. When your pictures are ready, study them, preferably with your model, and decide which ones are most satisfactory. Relate the results to the shape of your subject's face and see if you agree with our general guidelines discussed above. If you don't agree, see if you can arrive at a possible explanation for the difference.

---

### Review

**Now that we have discussed the fundamentals of studio lighting you will find it much easier to state where the key light has been placed in pictures. You should get into the habit of looking for shadows in other photographers' portraits and try working out**

Fig. 12.10 Effective use of fairly contrasty short lighting.

Fig. 12.11 Well-diffused broad lighting with plenty of fill-in has prevented shading of the eyes by the hat. Care was also taken to avoid undue highlights from the highly reflective earrings.

Fig. 12.12 Basically broad lighting but with less fill-in to suit this male character portrait. A slight tipping forward of the head has completely eliminated any reflection in the subject's glasses.

Fig. 12.13 Short lighting is used here to make the subject's face look thinner. An accent light adds some highlights.

**for yourself where the main light was likely to have been placed and see if you can discover the reason for its position. In some studio lighting set-ups, particularly where very diffused light sources have been used such as white nylon umbrellas, it can be quite difficult to discern the direction of the main light source as the shadows often are hardly visible. Nevertheless, the direction of the lighting is still of great importance and sets the general tone of the picture.**

**Diffused lighting is sometimes essential when taking portraits of, for example, girls wearing overhanging hair styles. If you are not careful, awkward shadows can appear on the subject's forehead. In professional studio set-ups, very large diffused light sources are often used. If you are faced with this sort of problem, try using an umbrella light source placed fairly low, as your main light, or even bounce your light off a white surface.**

As well as lighting there are a number of other ways to make your model look more attractive. Here are some features that can cause problems for the photographer and do not flatter the model. The solutions suggested in Table 12.1 show how you can improve certain situations.

A diffusion or soft focus filter can be very helpful in portraiture particularly when you are working with women whose wrinkles are beginning to show (see Chapter 5). Wrinkles in the skin can also be caused by the model's pose. Soft focus filters consist of concentric circles engraved on clear glass. They are available in several strengths and have their maximum effect at wide apertures.

Everything we have discussed so far applies equally well to tungsten lighting or electronic flash. Studio electronic flash units are much more expensive than floodlamps, but they do have some advantages. Floodlamps are bright and hot and models sometimes find it uncomfortable to sit in front of them for more than a short time. Overrun photoflood lamps are particularly unpleasant from this point of view, although studio lamps such as Photo Pearl are much better.

**Table 12.1** Suggested solutions to photographic problems

| Problem | Solution |
|---|---|
| Prominent nose | Turn the model's face directly towards the camera |
| Double chin | Raise the main light or tilt chin forward, or use a higher camera position |
| Glasses casting a shadow on the eyes and/or reflecting the light | Ask subject to tip face forward slightly by lowering the chin |
| Deep set eyes producing dark shadows | A lower key light and more diffused lighting |
| Overhanging hair styles | Lower main light and use more diffused light (as discussed above) |
| Bald head | Use a lower than normal camera position and do not use accent light on the head |
| Prominent ears | Keep the ear nearest the camera in shadow by using short lighting |
| Various facial defects | Try to keep on shadow side of the face |
| Wrinkles and facial blemishes | Use a lower key light, more diffused lighting, soft focus filter |

## Review

**Studio electronic flash units have low power modelling lights that can be used when setting up. The modelling lights are placed in the reflectors very close to the flash tubes themselves so that the light that they produce is similar in quality and direction to the flash. They can be used, therefore, in setting up to assess the shadow. As they are low power, they contribute nothing to the exposure or the colour balance. Studio electronic flash produces a light which is very similar in colour balance to daylight, so daylight balanced colour transparency film should be used.**

As we have already mentioned, studio electronic flash fitted with umbrellas are useful studio light sources and are capable of giving excellent results.

## The portrait session

When you set out to take portraits, there are three things to do:

- establish a happy atmosphere
- pose the model
- take the picture

For good results you need to provide a pleasant environment and establish a good relationship with your subject. For the beginner this is not always easy. It needs practice. Remember your model is human and so likes to be complimented, reassured and treated politely.

Prepare the studio so that you have your lights and background set up for the first of the arrangements you intend to use, and have your camera loaded with film and close at hand. If you intend to use a tripod, have the camera mounted on it and ready to use. Make sure the correct lens is fitted. Make sure that the studio conditions are comfortable for the model, that the studio is not too cold and that a mirror is available. Have something suitable for the model to sit on and have it placed at least 4 or 5 ft from the background. A stool is ideal. Chairs are often too low and have a back which can appear in your pictures. Make sure that the stool allows your model to place his or her feet on the floor and that it has a foot rest so that the model can sit comfortably.

When your model arrives it is worth spending a few minutes chatting to put both of you at ease. Offer a cup of tea or coffee or a soft drink. After a few minutes ask your model to sit on the stool and start taking pictures. If this is a new experience for the model you will probably find that the first few pictures turn out looking a little stiff and strained. You might be lucky enough to get one or two good pictures but usually the first half dozen or so can be written off. However, they will give your model time to settle.

It is discouraging to a sitter to work with a silent photographer, or one who occasionally grunts 'turn to the left', 'look this way', 'look to the right'. A good photographer will always compliment the model on his or her appearance and how he or she looks in individual photographs. Male and female models like to be flattered and told that they look good, so comments like these will help produce a relaxed and happy atmosphere and your pictures will be better as a result. A little music from a radio or tape recorder can also be helpful in establishing a relaxed atmosphere.

For best results remember the comfort of your model. Do not expect an uncomfortable pose to be held for long.

Your model will feel more comfortable if you ask him or her to pose with legs crossed. The crossed-over leg should be the one nearest the camera. This will also help to get a good postural position. If the model's hands rest naturally in his or her lap, a very relaxed pose will develop.

Up to this point we have discussed positioning the model and lights for head and shoulders or perhaps, three-quarter-length views. When taking full-length portraits you will need a wider background further back from your subject in order to get an even light coverage over the whole figure and to avoid troublesome shadows.

When using a 90-mm lens on a 35-mm camera, you will need to be almost 16 ft from an adult model in order to include the full height. Not many home studios have enough room. Also, remember you will need to place the model 4 to 6 ft in front of the background. By using a wide-angle lens you can get nearer. A 50-mm lens will place the camera about 9 ft away, and at this distance you will have no need to worry about perspective distortion.

A full-face pose, just as in head and shoulders portraiture, is not usually as attractive as when the face is at a slight angle to the camera. It is better to have the subject turned approximately 45 degrees from the camera. Legs will look best if the leg nearest the camera is pointed to face directly at the camera with the other leg slightly behind. Most of the body weight should rest on the back leg. The leg in front can be slightly bent at the knee. This position usually produces the most attractive results.

In head and shoulders portraiture, we do not normally need to consider hands, but in three-quarter- or full-length views, hands are important. Models often put their hands in very awkward, stiff positions. One good way of getting your model to relax the hands is to ask him or her to give them a good shake and then let them fall naturally.

Alternatively, let the hands do something. A girl could be holding a flower or a man a pipe. There are no firm rules about posing hands but do check the hands in your viewfinder and see if they look attractive and natural. Make sure they do not appear unduly large, stiff or prominent. Perhaps most important of all, never allow your subject to clasp the hands. Interlaced fingers always look like a bunch of bananas and can easily ruin an otherwise good pose.

Always take plenty of photographs during a portrait session. For each pose take at least three or four pictures because it is very common for a model's eyes to blink just as the shutter opens. Ask

There are two useful rules for successful portraiture.

**Focus on the eye nearest the camera.**
We always look into a person's eyes when we first meet and focus attention on the eye nearest us. We expect the same degree of focus in a picture and feel disturbed if the eye nearest us is not sharp. So always focus on the eye nearest the camera. There are very few autofocus cameras capable of selective focus to such a degree that they will concentrate on an eye in a face and focus on it. Therefore, manual focus is to be recommended in close-up portraits.

**Check small details before taking the picture.**
In taking any photograph it is good practice to check that there are no disturbing elements that can easily be removed. If your background is narrow, be especially careful if you move the camera position from one side of the model to the other, because the edge of the background can easily appear in your picture and you will not notice it until the prints are made. Check for wisps of hair out of place, make-up that is not quite correct, earrings which may be too big, distracting or reflecting light, or unattractive folds in clothing. Look particularly for small bits of tissue or anything white because these will be sure to stand out in the finished photograph.

**Fig. 12.14** A transparent umbrella is an unusual and attractive prop for this portrait.

**Fig. 12.15** This profile portrait is almost backlit and the cigarette smoke against the black background produces an interesting and unusual effect. (Photo: Kim Sawyer.)

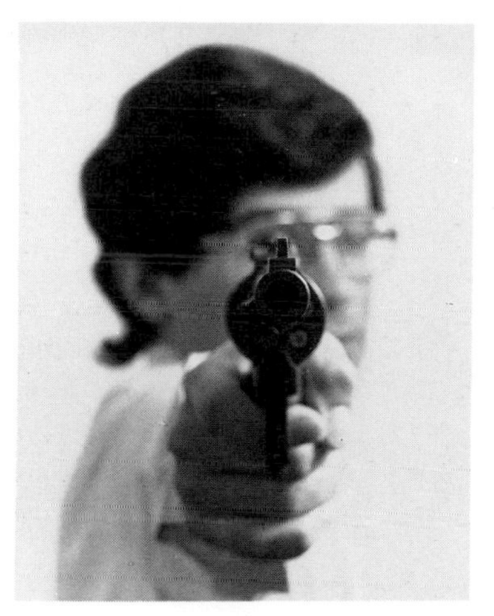

**Fig. 12.16** 'The Marksman'. One time when the rule that the eye nearest the camera should be sharp has been broken to spectacular effect. (Photo: J.B. Wayne.)

the model to change positions slightly between sets of pictures. All that is needed is a slight movement of the head.

---

## Exercise

Now you are ready to try a portrait session. Use a basic two-light set-up and take a number of head and shoulders portraits. Experiment with slight alterations in the position of the head, then move back a little and try some three-quarter- and full-length photographs. When the pictures have been processed, study each picture critically and pick out those in which the pose looks awkward and uncomfortable and decide how the model's position could be improved. Note carefully those poses which give the most satisfactory results.

---

Unless you are preparing a set for a character study, props (see Figures 12.14–12.16) should always be kept to a minimum and you should choose them carefully to help express the feel of your picture: a young lady could be holding a flower or, possibly, wearing an attractive hat.

Group photography is taking a portrait of two people or more. Special kinds of group photography include those where everyone is lined up in rows all looking at the camera. A school photograph, a football team or guests at a wedding are examples. A primary rule of photography is to have a single centre of interest, so as soon as you have more than one person in a picture, problems arise.

Try to aim for unity in your group pictures. Portraits of a small group of people are often more effective as head and shoulders pictures or three-quarter-length views. When photographing two people, a man and a woman for example, try to keep your subjects the same distance from the camera. If you do not, the head of the person nearest the camera can look too big. As a general rule try to have the man a little higher than the woman. This is nothing to do with status but simply the relative physical size we expect to see between male and female human subjects (Figure 12.17).

Try to ensure that the heads are together and separated by no more than three inches. Both subjects can be looking directly at the camera or at each other. If they are looking in different directions out of the picture, then the photograph will appear confused.

When taking larger groups try to get a feeling of unity even then (see Figure 12.18). If the people are looking in different directions, this can be very distracting and everyone should be asked either to look at the camera or to look at one person who then becomes the centre of interest. A family group taken on Mother's Day could turn out well with mother sitting on a couch or chair with the smaller children close to her or in her lap and other members of the family posed around her as close as possible, with no obvious gap between any of them.

## Location portraiture

Taking portraits on location is to do with photographing people in their own environment. This can show people at home, people enjoying a hobby or sport, people in their place of work, etc.

Fig. 12.17 A good example of a well-unified double portrait. The heads are close together and the arms form a pleasing circular line.

Fig. 12.18 A well-posed group picture of a tug-of-war team. Perhaps the composition could have been improved by closing up the gap between the second and third players in the back row and making sure that the trainer on the right was also looking at the camera. (Photo: Kim Sawyer.)

Fig. 12.19 An excellent location portrait showing a businessman in his office. (Photo: Kim Sawyer.)

A location portrait is at its best when it expresses the personality of the subject and the subject's interests or work. The basic rules or guidelines of good composition apply in location portraiture as elsewhere, so keep your photographs as simple as possible. Make sure there are no obviously distracting elements in the background and move in close so that your subject is the most important element in the scene. Close-up portraits are possible although usually three-quarter-length views are most effective. Full-length views can also work well. Make sure that the surroundings of your subject are fairly simple and avoid any bright areas that will distract attention from the subject.

The very best location portraits show the personality and interests of the subject (see Figures 12.19–12.21). A person who likes reading should be shown against a bookshelf with a book in his or her hand.

**Fig. 12.20** A location portrait showing an author in his study.

**Fig. 12.21** A behind-the-scenes location shot of actresses in their dressing-room making up for the show.

It would not be enough to show your subject against a plain background holding a book.

Your lighting for location portraits should be as simple as possible. Use available light whenever possible. Reflectors are very useful to reduce contrast and to fill in shadows. When using artificial light for location portraiture, make sure it is well diffused. Try not to use direct on-camera flash. Bounce flash is much better and if you can use an electronic flash with an umbrella or diffusing light box, lighting will be even better.

Available light usually means rather low light levels, so fast film is needed. For black and white location portraiture, Ilford XP2 rated at ISO 400/27 is very useful because it has an extremely wide latitude and can often show details in the shadows when other films fail. ISO 200/24 or ISO 400/27 colour film can also be used but, of course, latitude will be much less than even conventional black and white films.

The same rules for taking pictures of people at home apply for location portraiture at work. Set up the portrait so that the person is shown in the act of doing something related to his or her work. A secretary could be seated at his or her typewriter or word processor actually typing. Move in close and try to take a three-quarter- rather than a full-length view unless a full-length shot cannot be avoided. Move in even closer if your subjects are doing delicate work with their hands, such as jewellers or modelmakers.

Make sure there is plenty of light on the subject's face and as a rule the face should be the main centre of interest.

---

### Exercise

You should now take a series of location portraits. These can include pictures of people enjoying their hobbies or at work. Vary your view points and include close-up portraits, three-quarter- and full-length views. Try to use available light whenever possible. When the pictures are processed, select those you consider most successful. The model should always be the centre of interest, but the background too, while taking second place, is nevertheless important because it provides the viewer with information about the subject.

---

## Outdoor portraits

Outdoor portraits are among the most popular of all pictures. Most people start by taking pictures of family and friends out of doors. The main problems are:

- being too far away from your subject
- having confusing backgrounds

In outdoor portraiture, backgrounds are of prime importance. You should always check your background first. Look out for obvious difficulties like lamp-posts which might grow out of your subject's head. In beach scenes look out for the horizon line going in one ear of your subject and coming out the other. Take care in choosing your background. You can also use a wide aperture on your lens which will limit depth of field and so throw confusing backgrounds

Fig. 12.22 This outdoor location portrait of a photographer at a race meeting nicely places the subject in his environment. (Photo: Leica Camera Ltd.)

well out of focus. Attention to details like these will make all the difference between a successful picture and a failure.

You should take advantage of the outdoor environment (Figure 12.22) and use opportunities to frame your subject against a suitable background (Figure 12.23).

Daylight is the main light source but you may still need to use reflectors or possibly fill-in flash to make sure there is enough light on your subject's face. This can be very important in colour photography. For most subjects, avoid taking pictures in direct,

Fig. 12.23 An interesting outdoor portrait in which the costumed subject is nicely placed against a suitable background. (Photo: Kim Sawyer.)

Rim lighting can also be used in the studio to produce halo lighting effects around the hair. The simplest way to do this is to position a small light source, such as a spotlight, immediately behind your subject. When taking your picture, make sure that no part of the spotlight or stand is visible in your viewfinder and that all the equipment is hidden behind the model.

bright sunlight. Not only will the result be contrasty but the subject will find it hard on the eyes. Diffused, hazy sunlight or even an overcast day will provide ideal lighting for outdoor portraiture both in black and white and in colour. Taking portraits against the light can be most effective, especially if the sun behind the subject produces attractive rim lighting on the head. Rim lighting is a bright halo of lighting around the head caused by the sun being behind it. Rim lighting sharply separates the head from the background. You will need to increase your exposure by one stop at least so that the face does not appear too dark. Reflectors or fill-in flash can also be used to lighten the face.

## Exercise

You can now try some outdoor head and shoulders portraits. Use the same rules as we discussed about shadows and the main light source in studio portraiture and try to apply those rules in the outdoor situation. Use a reflector or fill-in flash if it is necessary to lighten dark shadows. Also try to reduce any distractions in the background by putting them out of focus or by trying to choose simple backgrounds.

## Child portraiture

Portraiture of children should be approached in exactly the same way as taking pictures of adults. Older children can be posed and will follow directions. Younger ones are not so easy to take and best results will usually be obtained if the parent is on hand. Try to avoid looking down on the child, and if you lower the camera to be level with the child's face, best results will be obtained.

Mother and child can make charming portraits. Do take care, however, that your picture does not show two separate individuals becoming two separate centres of interest. Remember to keep faces close together and make sure that the baby is not looking at something off camera while the mother is looking straight at the lens. Mother and baby looking at one another can make a most attractive portrait.

## Character portraiture

Portraits of people made up to represent fictional characters can be most interesting and rewarding. At one time this was a most popular form of portraiture. If you are in touch with an amateur theatrical group you could have a source of wonderful models. Remember to pose them in suitable surroundings.

## Portraits of animals

The main consideration for taking successful portraits of human subjects are just as applicable when we photograph animals. The basic guidelines of simplicity, moving in close and focusing on the eye nearest the camera, are all valid (Figure 12.24).

People can be asked to assume a pose and stand in a particular spot. Most animals are not so obliging. In the studio, a pet can be coaxed to pose with food but can quickly lose interest. You need patience and sometimes you need to wait a long time for an interesting photograph. You must be prepared to take plenty of pictures.

Outdoors the same considerations apply. Take your time, be patient and be prepared to take lots of pictures. Domestic animals and pets can usually be approached without too much trouble. However, other animals can be shy or dangerous. You often require longer focal length lenses than you would for human subjects. At the zoo there can be obstacles such as netting and bars, but these can often be eliminated or reduced by using the widest possible aperture on your lens and photographing the subject as closely as possible.

Wild birds and animals sometimes need special techniques and a

**Fig. 12.24** Animal portraiture follows the same rules as photographing people. This is a 13-year-old Macaque monkey from Java.

'hide' may need to be constructed. This is a specialist area of photography and the interested reader is referred to the book *All About Photographing Animals and Birds* by David Hodgson, published by Pelham Books.

## Further Reading

*Lighting for Portraiture* by Walter Nurnberg, published by Focal Press.
*Studio Techniques in Portrait Photography*, published by Eastman Kodak, USA.
*Picturing People for Pleasure & Profit* by John Wade, published by the Bureau of Freelance Photographers.
*People in My Camera* by Michael Gnade, published by Focal Press.

## Summary

**In this chapter we have dealt with the fundamentals of portraiture and have discussed how to take successful studio, location and outdoor portraits.**

---

# 13 Press Photography and Photojournalism

When you have completed this chapter you will be able to prepare photographs suitable for reproduction in newspapers and magazines and prepare and write suitable captions for those pictures. You will also understand how to prepare a photo essay.

Press Photography and Photojournalism is the production of photographs which will be reproduced in one form or another on the printed page. This includes newspapers, magazines, reports of various kinds, books and booklets, postcards, leaflets and posters. Indeed, any printed material which is reproduced in relatively large numbers and which uses the half-tone method of reproduction.

Ink is used in the printing process. Because of this it is not really a practical proposition to reproduce photographs, containing a full range of tones, using ink. The reason is that there are serious technical problems involved in controlling the amount of ink and its density in the kind of way that would give a similar result to a photograph. This problem is overcome by breaking the image up into a large number of very small dots. Plates for use in the printing process are produced by re-photographing the picture through a special dot screen. These dots on the surface of the printing plate are then used to transfer ink to the printing paper. Because the dots on the printing plate are inked, the larger the dots and the greater their number, the more ink is transferred to the paper and the darker

---

## Exercise

Using a reasonably powerful magnifying glass, have a close look at a photograph reproduced in a newspaper. You will clearly see the dot pattern and you will notice how the dots increase in size in the darker areas and are smaller in the light areas. In a newspaper the pattern is fairly coarse but high-quality magazine reproduction the dot screen is much finer and a larger number of dots are used. Now look at a photograph with the magnifying glass in one of the high-quality glossy magazines. You will clearly see how very much finer the dot pattern appears.

---

becomes the area. The smaller the dots carrying the ink, and the fewer, the lighter the area.

In the reproduction of colour on the printed page, the half-tone process is also used. The underlying principle is virtually the same as the subtractive colour process described in Chapter 11. In straightforward colour reproduction, the original photograph is re-photographed in black and white several times. In the simplest form of colour reproduction, it is photographed using red, blue and green filters. The resulting black and white negatives are called colour separations. As before, a dot pattern is superimposed. These colour separations are used to prepare a set of printing plates. The paper is run through the press once for each colour and the images are printed in exact register, one on top of the other. The inks used in printing are the complementary colours, magenta, cyan and yellow. When these are viewed on the printed page, they remove appropriate colours from white light and so reproduce the original colours of the original scene. A full description of the subtractive process of colour reproduction appears in Chapter 11, page 150. The complementary colours in the case of the printed page are, of course, coloured inks whereas in the colour photograph they are dyes. In most colour printing in magazines and newspapers, a fourth run through is done using black ink which gives an extra 'bite' to the finished picture. In very high quality graphic art printing rather more runs are made through the printing press, using different coloured inks.

## Exercise

Using the same magnifying glass, have a look at, firstly, a colour photograph reproduced in a newspaper; and, secondly, a colour photograph appearing in a good-quality glossy magazine. You should be able to see clearly the difference between the two sizes of dots and you should also be able to see quite clearly, specially in the newspaper illustration, the magenta, cyan and yellow dots.

## Pictures for reproduction

In order to be considered for reproduction in the press, a photograph needs to reach certain minimum technical standards. The picture should be correctly exposed to have good detail in shadow and highlight areas. Print quality must be good – that is, there should be a good range of tones between pure black and pure white, and it should be of good contrast range. When a printing plate is produced, contrast tends to increase. If your print is a little on the soft side, therefore, the printer can increase contrast but is not able to reduce it easily.

Usually, the print size expected is 8 × 10 in. Slightly smaller prints are acceptable but these should not be less than 6 × 8 in. Sometimes it is possible to submit smaller size prints but this can only be done when you have established a relationship with an editor and size requirements of the pictures have been discussed and agreed.

There is one exception to the quality rule and that is if the picture has such overriding news importance that quality is a secondary consideration. An example is the photographs taken when President John F. Kennedy was assassinated.

## Composition of Photographs for publication

Unless the subject of a news picture is extremely important, good composition is often the factor deciding whether or not a picture will be published. The basic guidelines of good composition, which we discussed in Chapter 1, are particularly important in preparing photographs for the press. The most memorable pictures – those that tend to be reproduced again and again – have very strong composition, and as a great deal of news is related to people, people should be very prominent in your photographs and faces should nearly always be clearly visible.

## Exercise

Obtain a selection of newspapers and magazines. Go through them very carefully examining in detail each photograph which appears. Apply to them the basic photographic guidelines we have described in Chapter 1 and see if you could improve the picture still further. Most of the pictures will have been substantially cropped, of course, as space is always at a premium on the printed page.

## Colour pictures for reproduction

All that we have said about black and white pictures regarding quality and composition applies equally well to colour photographs submitted for publication.

Most publications prefer colour transparencies (slides) to colour prints. There are exceptions, however, in that colour prints showing events of exceptional interest or news value will be used. The reason for this preference is that it is usually much easier to make good colour separations from slides than from colour prints. However, new technology is fast closing the gap and greater use is now being made of good-quality colour prints.

### Review

**Photographs are reproduced in the press by the half-tone process. Pictures are broken up into a pattern of microscopic dots which enable the full range of tones in a photograph to be reproduced by the printing process. Prints from reproduction in the press should be of good technical quality, printed on glossy paper and be of a minimum size of usually of 6 × 8 in. The better the composition of a photograph the more chance it has to be reproduced. Colour photographs should be submitted as slides rather than colour prints. Minimum size is 35 mm but magazines prefer larger format transparencies.**

# News pictures

## Hot news photographs

Major events are unpredictable. Accidents, disasters, air crashes, assassinations, terrorist attacks or a streaker at a national sports event can occur anywhere at anytime. If you happen to be on the spot with a camera and get pictures of such an event, you can probably make a lot of money. This is why any would-be press photographer should always carry a camera. Today many small compact cameras taking 35-mm film can easily be carried in a pocket. They can be an excellent investment not only to take hot news pictures but to take other interesting shots as well (see later).

If you should happen to be present at some newsworthy event, you should take as many photographs as you possibly can and should move in as close as you can so that you can record the faces of the people involved. You should also collect names and addresses of any people you photograph, if this is possible. If the event is of national interest, do not waste time developing and printing your pictures. You should telephone at once one of the national newspapers and ask to speak to the Picture Editor or the News Desk. Describe the pictures you have taken and ask if the paper is interested. If they are you will be told what to do next. This will usually be to send the film direct to the newspaper by courier or by passenger train. The paper will process and print your pictures and use them if they are of sufficient interest, and may arrange syndication to other newspapers also. Of course, you hold the copyright of your pictures and if the event is sufficiently newsworthy you stand to gain very substantial reproduction fees.

## Local news events

Local news is rather different. In your neighbourhood there are many events worth photographing. Some of these should be of interest to the local press or even to the national press or magazines. Some famous person or a member of the royal family may visit. (A typical example is seen in Figure 13.1.) Or you may take pictures at your local beauty contest or carnival. In these kinds of situations

Fig. 13.1 The Queen visits. A typical news picture of both national and local interest. (Photo: Keith Hawkins.)

you should develop and print the pictures yourself and send them to the local press. At present the local free newspapers can provide a useful outlet for the work of freelance photographers. When sending pictures to the local press they must always be accompanied by suitable captions.

## Captions

The caption you submit with your photographs should preferably be typed and firmly attached to the back of the photograph. Also on the back of the photograph should be the name of the photographer, with address and telephone number.

Fig. 13.2

Your caption should contain a minimum of five essential points. These are often called the 'Five Ws'. They are: **Who**, **What**, **Where**, **When**, **Why**.

An editor may not publish all these facts but needs to know them in order to decide whether or not to use your photographs. Figure 13.2 is a good example.

A caption for this figure reading simply 'Douglas Hurd visits an electrical factory' would be wholly inadequate. A more suitable caption could read something like 'Douglas Hurd, the Foreign Secretary, (*who*) being shown the production line (*what*) on a visit to the NALCO factory (*where*) on February 22nd (*when*) just after the factory had won a substantial order from General Motors for the supply of electrical equipment (*why*).' The caption could be further improved by naming the other people in the picture.

In local news pictures, names and addresses of people appearing in the picture are particularly important for the editor knows that sales of the paper will increase if local people appear in pictures and are named.

When submitting pictures to the press you should always use cardboard-backed envelopes or enclose a stiffener to prevent damage in transit. Enclose a stamped, self-addressed envelope if you want your pictures returned. Fees vary, and local newspapers are not

Fig. 13.3 An amusing bit of graffiti seen on Brighton Station.

renowned for their generosity. You should always enclose a short note saying that you are offering the paper single reproduction rights of your pictures at their usual rate. This will establish that you expect a fee for your work and that you are offering one time reproduction rights only.

## Feature photographs

Many newspapers and magazines publish photographs which are not strictly speaking news but have some interesting, unusual or amusing aspect. Notices and clever graffiti are examples. Figure 13.3 is an example of such a photograph that has been sold to a number of different papers.

Figure 13.4 is a good clear picture of an injured football player receiving emergency treatment on the field. This could be either a news picture naming the individuals in the caption or simply a feature picture with a caption about care of injured players.

Fig. 13.4 An injured football player gets first aid on the field. (Photo: Keith Hawkins.)

Fig. 13.5 Amusing animal pictures can be appealing and can find a ready market.

Fig. 13.6 Nina Falaise – the deaf ballerina.

Animals in unusual situations or doing unlikely things can also find a ready market, as this picture of a typing cat (Figure 13.5). Such shots often appeal to editors.

## Photo essays

The practice of using photographs to help tell a specific story is known as photojournalism. Photo essays, also often called picture stories, can take a variety of forms. In its simplest form a photo essay consists of one picture with a suitable caption and some accompanying text. Figure 13.6, which is a typical example, is an action shot of the ballerina Nina Falaise. Her story is interesting because she happens to be completely deaf. This picture, or perhaps two or three pictures of Nina, could accompany a short article on how she has overcome the handicap of deafness.

Fig. 13.7 Using a crochet hook to remove a negative strip from a negative filing system.

Figure 13.7, which shows an ordinary crochet hook being used to remove a strip of negatives from a negative file, is the only illustration needed to accompany a 'do-it-yourself' article on care of negatives suitable for a photographic magazine.

Hobby magazines present many opportunities for the would-be photojournalist to prepare photo essays which have a good chance of publication if they are angled to appeal to the readership of those magazines. Figures 13.8–13.11 show a typical series of photographs which might be used to illustrate an article for a horticultural magazine, showing how to set up an avocado stone in a hydroculture medium.

Figure 13.8 is an establishing shot showing everything necessary to carry out the operation. The caption of this photograph could list the items shown in the picture. Figure 13.9 shows the avocado stone and its root system, Figure 13.10 shows the stone being placed in the special hydroculture pot and the holding medium being added, and Figure 13.11 shows the finished job. A short article would accompany these pictures and their captions.

Fig. 13.8 Everything needed to pot up an avocado stone in hydroculture medium.

Fig. 13.9 Close-up view of the avocado stone and root system.

Fig. 13.10 Inserting the plant in the pot. The clay granules are used as a support instead of soil.

Fig. 13.11 The finished article being lowered into its decorative container.

## Exercise

Choose a simple set of operations such as putting together a simple plastic toy or model kit or changing the batteries of a transistor radio or calculator. Photograph the main stages of this procedure. Put together the pictures in their correct sequence. Write a short introductory note and captions to the pictures. Show this photo essay to a friend and ask him or her whether in his or her opinion it shows clearly how to do the operation. This is a very good way of starting to produce photo essays.

More ambitious photo essays can be undertaken on almost any subject. So far we have talked about simpler subjects or 'how to . . .' subjects; however, photo essay possibilities are all around us.

Some examples are 'Leisure opportunities for young people in a small market town', 'Children at play', 'A visit to a race meeting', etc. Other possibilities exist such as 'A day in the life of . . .'. A photo essay could show a day in the life of a nurse, a plumber, a traffic warden or perhaps a teacher. Alternatively, some interesting activity in your area could be covered such as a local group clearing up an amenity area or a polluted stream.

Our next set of photographs show a photo essay about the inventor of a small economy car. The idea came from a single picture and short caption published in a local paper. The photographer then followed up the lead, approached the inventor and arranged to take a series of pictures.

Figure 13.12 shows Dr Jephcott of Fairwarp in Sussex with the prototype of the small three-wheel car he had invented. This picture has the advantage of showing Dr Jephcott, his invention and a feature of the invention, namely its tipping capabilities. Note how much more interesting this photograph is when compared with a straightforward shot of the vehicle by itself (Figure 13.13).

Figure 13.14 is a close-up of the special tipping mechanism.

If a photo essay contains more than two or three pictures, it is

Fig. 13.12 Dr Jephcott demonstrating his prototype three-wheel car.

Fig. 13.13 The prototype three-wheel car.

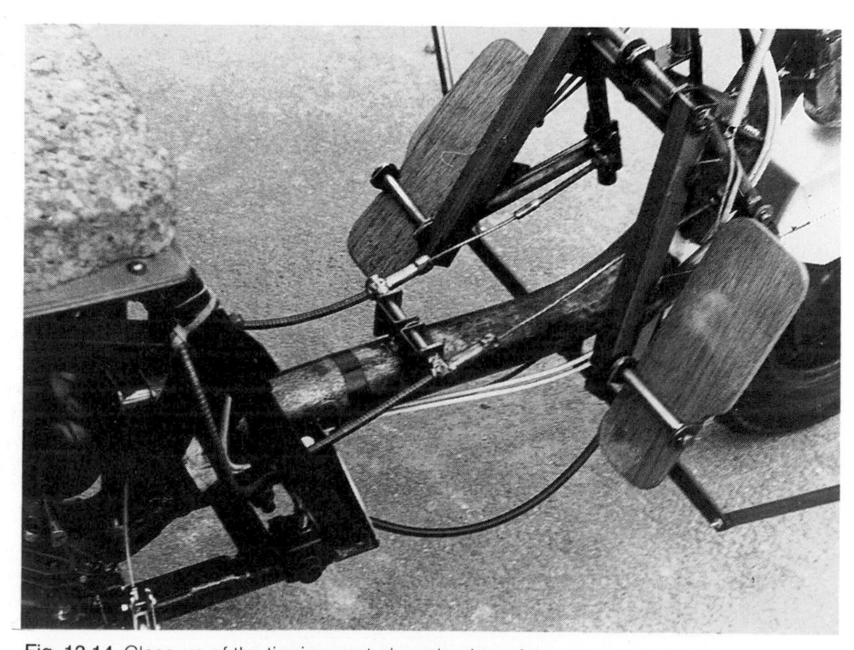

Fig. 13.14 Close-up of the tipping control mechanism of the prototype three-wheel car.

Fig. 13.15 Dr Jephcott's production prototype car.

important to vary the viewpoints and a close-up is always interesting and informative. The production prototype of Dr Jephcott's car is shown in Figure 13.15. It would be an advantage to have a person in this picture and, whether we regard it as politically correct or not, that person could be a girl. Whether we like it or not, a fact of life is that girls sell products and editors like them.

An interesting example is the experience of *Amateur Photographer*. At one time, in *AP*'s editorial office there was a chart relating subject matter on the front cover to sales. These always peaked when a girl appeared on the cover compared with landscapes, animals, sports personalities, etc. Research showed that this was really nothing to do with the potential reader wanting to look lecherously at a collection of 'girly' pictures. It acted, however, as a 'hook' to make the potential buyer pick up the magazine in a newsagent's shop. Once in the reader's hand the sale is virtually made because on flipping through the pages interest easily becomes centred on an article about testing some new product or how to photograph some tricky subject. This tactic works with potential women readers as well as men. Just look at the subjects on the cover of magazines such as *Woman* and *Woman's Own*.

Finally, one or two action shots of the car should be included (Figures 13.16 and 13.17).

Since the photographs will be accompanied by a short article, each photograph will not require as detailed a caption as would be

Fig. 13.16 The three-wheel car in action.

Fig. 13.17 The three-wheel car making a sharp turn.

necessary for single news photographs. The five Ws will not necessarily be required. Captions in a photo essay should not repeat what is actually seen in the picture but can be used to add additional information and help to promote the story.

---

## Exercise

Choose a subject that interests you in your area. Perhaps the effects of pollution in a local river would prove rewarding. The possible topics are endless and are limited only by your imagination. However, you should initially choose one that is fairly easy to carry out and produce a photo essay.

You will need to research the subject carefully, decide what pictures you would like to take and, if necessary, obtain permission to take them. Make all necessary arrangements then go out and take your pictures. Remember to take as many pictures as you possibly can and from those make your final selection. Vary your viewpoints and, needless to say, make careful notes of what you have taken. Put these together in the form of a photo essay and send it to a suitable publication.

---

## Finding possible markets

The aspiring photojournalist will find many markets listed in *Writers' and Artists' Year Book*. This indispensable publication appears in the autumn of each year and is published by A&C Black, London.

The Bureau of Freelance Photographers at Focus House, 479 Green Lanes, London N13 4PB, also publish a Market Handbook and additionally produce for their members a monthly Newsletter containing the most up-to-date information on possible markets for freelance photographers. Their service is highly recommended.

For photographers and writers, *Freelance Market News* published by Freelance Press Services, Cumberland House, Lissadale Street, Salford M6 6GG, is also a highly recommended publication.

## Further Reading

To see how photo essays have been tackled, two particular books are well worth reading:

*Picture Post 1938–1950*, edited by Tom Hopkinson, published by Penguin.
*Great Photographic Essays from Life*, published by the New York Graphic Society.

## Summary

**In this chapter we have discussed press photography, photojournalism and photo essays. A description has been given of the basic principles of reproduction on the printed page and the preparation of photographs suitable for reproduction. The difference between hot news and local news has been described and details have been given on how to submit pictures to both the national and local press. The art of picture captioning has also been described in detail.**

**The differences between news, general interest and feature pictures have been described and the nature of picture story or photo essay has been discussed. Details have also been given on how to prepare a 'do-it-yourself' picture story and picture stories on other subjects. Suggestions have been given on how to submit pictures and picture stories to the editors of publications.**

# Appendix

In the preceding chapters we have covered the most popular City & Guilds 9231 modules. A considerable number of others are available. However, by no means all will necessarily be taught at your chosen centre. You may well need to shop around. The following other modules are all in the advanced category.

9231–031 Art of Black and White Photography
9231–032 Exhibition Photographic Printing
9231–033 Image Derivation
9231–034 Images without Lenses

9231–041 Art of Colour Photography
9231–042 Negative/Positive Colour Printing
9231–043 Reversal Colour Printing

9231–051 Landscape
9231–052 Still Life
9231–053 Buildings

9231–061 Social Documentary Photography (mentioned in Chapter 13)
9231–062 Constructed Images

9231–070 Close-up
9231–071 Natural History
9231–072 Action and Movement
9231–073 Macrophotography

9231–080 Tape-slide
9231–081 Introduction to Video Photography
9231–082 Video Production

9231–090 Introduction to the History of Photography
9231–091 Architectural Photography
9231–092 Record Photography
9231–093 View Camera Photography

In addition, at the time of writing, City & Guilds have in preparation other new modules which will be introduced from time to time.

Prospective candidates are always advised to consult the current official City & Guilds scheme booklets which contain syllabus details of all available modules, including details of new ones and changes which may have been made in existing modules.

In addition, of course, to the practical presentation, all submissions *must* be accompanied by the workbook and self-evaluation which we have fully discussed in previous chapters. The booklets can be obtained from the City & Guilds of London Institute, Publications Section, 76 Portland Place, London W1N 4AA, telephone 0171-278-2468. A 'phone call before ordering is advised to ascertain exactly which booklet you require and the current charge.

## Licentiateship of the Royal Photographic Society

City & Guilds in cooperation with the Royal Photographic Society operate a scheme whereby students gaining good passes in five City & Guilds 9231 modules will be automatically awarded the Licentiateship of the Royal Photographic Society on application to that body.

The conditions are that candidates must have taken five City & Guilds 9231 modules and in so doing scored a minimum of 11 points. Points are awarded as follows: a Distinction gains 3 points, a Credit gains 2 points and a Pass gains 1 point. At least one Distinction must have been obtained by the candidate but this cannot be in Starting Photography, Photo Essay or Social Documentary Photography. These modules do score 3 points if a Distinction is gained but the obligatory Distinction must be in one of the other modules.

Prospective candidates are advised to contact City & Guilds or the

Royal Photographic Society to ascertain the most up-to-date requirements as these regulations are subject to revision and change.

## Submission for CGLI 9231–020

Chapters 1–8 of this book cover everything needed to make a submission for examination in the City & Guilds 9231 Starting Photography module. Your tutor will have already discussed with you just what City & Guilds require. The photographic work essentially divides into two parts. In the first you are asked to carry out a short photographic 'experiment' to demonstrate some aspect of a photographic technique. For instance our set of pictures in Chapter 3 showing the effect on pictures of a scene when focal lengths of lenses are changed could form the basis of an exercise. In Chapter 6 the exercise demonstrating the effect of using various colour filters on the subject (page 78) could be modified and used. Take care to state concisely at the beginning of your practical exercise precisely what you intend to demonstrate. As well as the set of pictures, brief notes on exactly what they show must be included.

In the second part of the submission, you are asked to take a series of pictures based on a theme. This could be something like 'Autumn', 'Water', 'Day in the life of a dog', etc. The possibilities are endless. Whatever you choose, however, make sure that you include a good variety of viewpoints, ranging from long views, medium views, close-ups and big close-ups. Remember City & Guilds want variety. They need to see that you can take pictures of various subjects in various circumstances, but with some central theme running through them such as the already mentioned 'Autumn'. Of course, your submission should be accompanied by your workbook and your self-evaluation, as discussed in the Introduction.

It is important to note the following: City & Guilds would like you to write *separate* self-evaluations of the two parts of your submission. That is, you should include a self-evaluation at the end of part one, the exercise demonstrating some aspect of photography technique, and a second self-evaluation should appear after your set of pictures on a theme. See the Introduction for a discussion on preparing a self-evaluation.

## Submission for CGLI 9231–030

Chapters 1–10 of this book cover everything needed to make a submission for the City & Guilds 9231 Introduction to Black and White Photography examination.

In this submission you must be able to demonstrate an ability to photograph a variety of subjects on black and white film material. You must also be able to demonstrate that you can satisfactorily process your own films and make satisfactory black and white enlargements from those films. This submission is suitable only for those who have access to darkroom facilities either at college, at home or elsewhere. (In some areas there are good darkroom facilities for hire and some camera clubs also have them for members' use.)

The City & Guilds submission calls for a minimum of five good black and white prints (however, we would recommend at least ten good prints to demonstrate a wide variety of subject matter). The workbook must also be included and it should contain examples of test strips and prints made from their recommendations and contact prints of *all* photographs taken for this module. The usual self-evaluation must also be included. Remember that City & Guilds do not like to see prints that are grey overall.

## Submission for CGLI 9231–040

Chapters 1–8 and 11 of this book cover all you require in background material to tackle a City & Guilds submission in the 9231 Introduction to Colour Photography module.

The minimum photographic submission is eight prints *or* slides but we do suggest more pictures should be submitted. Aim for around fifteen ideally. Do not submit a mixture of prints and slides. It is vital that a good variety of subject matter be included and it does help if these are on some sort of coherent theme. This could be something like 'Gardens' or 'The River' or perhaps even 'The City'. It is vital in this module that the *use* of colour is demonstrated. When you look at your pictures ask yourself if they would be as effective in black and white as they are in colour. If the answer is 'Yes' then they are not suitable for this submission. Colour must appear essential for your theme. The usual workbook must accompany your submission.

## Submission for CGLI 9231–050

Chapters 1–8 and 12 of this book will prepare you for submission of a portfolio for examination in the City & Guilds Portraiture module. This module is one which City & Guilds regard as being advanced; in other words, your background is assumed to be such that you could easily have passed any one of the introductory modules such as Starting Photography, Introduction to Black and White Photography or Introduction to Colour Photography. You will be expected to be able to produce, or have produced for you, good technical quality prints that are well composed. Your tutor will have discussed with you the kind of practical portfolio which City & Guilds require for the portraiture module. City & Guilds are looking for demonstration of your ability to take good portrait studies under a variety of conditions. We have found that at least fifteen photographs should be submitted. A good combination is three formal studio portraits, three location portraits and three outdoor portraits. The remaining six or so additional pictures could include photographs of children and animals and at least one or two groups. Always remember to concentrate on people in the pictures and keep reasonably close to your subject. Be wary of taking pictures outdoors in which the subject is too small and possibly has his or her back to the camera. This is fatal. Remember to present your pictures in an attractive manner. Also do remember the vital requirement that you must keep a workbook detailing aims, technical data, etc., for each picture and that this should accompany your submission.

## Submission for CGLI 9231–060

Chapters 1–8 and 13 of this book cover everything needed to make a submission for the City and Guilds 9231 Photo Essay module. This is an advanced module and the remarks we made previously in relation to Portraiture are also applicable to this submission.

The syllabus suggests that your photo essay should contain between eight and ten photographs on the subject of your choice. Your article can be quite short and your captions should be snappy and to the point.

In writing any short article to accompany a set of pictures, try to be brief. Remember to start with a striking sentence. In some ways this is one of the most important aspects of your photo essay. A good opening sentence can attract attention and make the reader continue reading. Your workbook should contain your notes on the planning and research of your project, and you should describe your subject treatment, your approach and an interpretation of the theme of your photo essay. As usual, your self-evaluation should be included.

For the City & Guilds 9231–061, Social Documentary Photography, candidates are expected to produce a photo essay which looks specifically at people and their social condition. Some of the greatest photo essays have been on precisely this subject. In addition to the photo essay, this module does require rather more reading and the candidate will need to write a fairly lengthy essay on the relationship of his or her own work to other workers in the field or on some aspect of the history of social documentary photography.

# Index